LAW

Real Stories of the Rattlesnake Lawyer

Jonathan Miller

Joanne
Enjoy
the
book!

Library of Congress Cataloging-in-Publication Data
Miller, Jonathan, (criminal defense lawyer) author
  Laws & loves : real stories of the rattlesnake lawyer / Jonathan Miller.
    pages cm
  ISBN 978-1-937240-41-7 (pbk.) -- ISBN 978-1-937240-34-9 (ebook) 1. Lawyers--New Mexico--Humor. 2. Law--New Mexico--Humor. 3. Lawyers--New Mexico--Anecdotes. I. Title.

  K184.M56 2014
  340.092--dc23

                            2014008509

20140320

Casa de Snapdragon LLC
12901 Bryce Avenue, NE
Albuquerque, NM 87112
http://www.casadesnapdragon.com
Printed in the United States of America

INTRODUCTION

"I always tell the truth, even when I lie."
Tony Montana.

Every word in this book is true, even the lies. As I now edit these stories at my office with its commanding view of downtown Albuquerque, I'm reading another man's life rather than my own. I no longer have perfect recall of these events and sometimes no recall at all. Is this collection fiction or non-fiction? As an attorney, I can argue that everything herein is substantially true by a preponderance of evidence, but definitely not true beyond a reasonable doubt.

Laws & Loves Part I is a collection merging two entries in the Southwest Writers non-fiction book proposal category. *Legal Lap Dances* won first prize and a few years later, *Law, Lust & Love* took second. I have also added some published and unpublished musings that have survived in the various nooks and crannies of my electronic files. Many of those publications no longer exist. Did publishing my works lead to their early demise? I'll take the fifth.

The stories in *Part I* focus on my young lawyer adventures, anything that occurred prior to my sabbatical from law to study the American Film Institute in Los Angeles at age thirty-six. My first novel, *Rattlesnake Lawyer* was published on the day I graduated from film school, and my life was never the same after that. I've included a few Hollywood stories from my first sojourn in LA, the spring quarter at UCLA Extension back when I was thirty-two. I then returned to Albuquerque and resumed practicing law for four more years and countless more stories.

During those years, I was looking for law and love in all the wrong places. A few stories in this collection actually occurred after I returned from LA the second time, but in those instances I still acted like a young lawyer. Thankfully, I am happily married now and settled down so I don't expect any more of the dating stories. Subsequent collections will deal with midlife and the law and how I finally put my foolish ways behind me. Yeah, right.

With regard to the cases and alleged criminals described in *Part I*, every name and detail has been changed to protect the innocent and the guilty alike. Just to be on the safe side, I have also changed the identities of the non-criminals. I am far more scared of the old girlfriends than the criminals, especially the ones who have become lawyers.

Still, I am confident to call this non-fiction, because while the particulars might be altered, all the emotions—the dreams and nightmares, the loves and losses—they are all very real. The triumphs and the tragedies are all mine, and they occurred much in the matter described even if the dates and details don't always match.

As I've said, I always tell the truth especially when I lie. Tony Montana would be proud.

CONTENTS

TALES OF A NOT SO BRAVE ULYSSES

Ulysses ended his odyssey in ancient Ithaca. My odyssey began in Ithaca New York, and has never ended. At twenty-two, I was a senior at Cornell returning from my final spring break back from the mythical land of Myrtle Beach. Hell had frozen over and then thawed into sulfur and brimstone slush. As I approached our mailbox in the aptly named Collegetown student ghetto, a chill ran through my gut. This would be the last return to Ithaca as an undergrad. In two months, I'd bust into adulthood like a bat out of Hades.

Unfortunately, the only way out of Ithaca was through the mailbox. After applying to several law schools, the replies waited for me as I broke off the icicles and pried open the mailbox door. One single acceptance letter would change my life—a golden ticket or a holy grail. My ultimate identity would be found inside one of the waiting envelopes and assorted utility bills.

My girlfriend, the Penelope to my Ulysses, decided to return to her place downtown and asked me to call her with the good news. "Surprise me," she said. She didn't say that the future of our relationship depended on where I ended up. She didn't have to.

My two roommates had already learned their fates from the admission gods while I pretended to relax on the beach. One had been accepted at Harvard, Yale, *and* Columbia as a safety school. He wanted to apply to the tiny, isolated University of Hawaii Law School as an out-of-state applicant, just to make sure that he could be accepted into *every* law school in America.

My other roommate was accepted into Michigan. He didn't hesitate to tell me, "I got into Michigan, what the hell do you know?" in his thick Long Island accent. "With your grades, you should have covered your ass and applied to Albany or Buffalo."

I didn't know how to respond, what the hell did I know indeed, but Albany or Buffalo? There was a reason I had gone to Myrtle Beach for spring break.

I stayed outside in the cold and opened the first letter, from Stanford. Three years in sunny Palo Alto sounded perfect right now. The opening sentence of the letter congratulated me on my outstanding achievement. Well thank you, Stanford. Hello, rest of my life. It took me two more sentences before the actual rejection part of the letter. Oh well, I wouldn't be a patent attorney for start-ups with stock options in the Bay Area. I saved the letter; it is still the nicest rejection I have ever received.

The second letter came from the University of Michigan, my roommate's alma mater to be. This was personal. Go Blue! Corporate law in the Midwest perhaps, with football tailgates every fall weekend didn't sound that bad either. I opened the letter so fast that the paper cut my finger.

Unfortunately, Michigan didn't bother to be nice in their terse letter stained by my blood. My finger and my heart had been clawed by a wolverine.

The upstate sun was setting and it grew colder and darker by the minute. I hurried into the cramped living room of my apartment, glad that my roommates weren't home to witness this. The next four letters said the same thing—the waitlist at Northwestern, Georgetown, Duke and North Carolina. One waitlist, I could understand, but four was inconceivable. Some of Ulysses' crew were forever stuck in the Land of the Lotus Eaters and never made it home. Would I be eating lotus for the rest of my life and never find a home of my own?

Where was my home anyway? I had spent my high school years in Albuquerque, but even though I'd been accepted into the University of New Mexico Law School, Albuquerque wasn't even an option. I had ended up in upstate New York for a reason, to escape New Mexico. Eric Clapton had sung a song called "Tales of the Brave Ulysses" back when he was with the band *Cream*, but I felt more like Bruce Springsteen singing about escaping his home town in *every* song of his early career. Returning to Albuquerque would be like Bruce playing the Stone Pony in Asbury Park for the rest of his life—*Born to Rust*.

A final envelope had fallen to the floor next to a pile of dirty underwear. I couldn't make out the smudged return address when tearing it open. "Tuition and fees are due at this date." It was from the University of Colorado Law School.

Colorado? The one in Boulder? Didn't I bounce a check to them? Of all the schools in the entire world, why did it have to be in Boulder?

According to Freud, there were no accidents in life. I had indeed bounced that check on purpose after splurging on three deluxe pizzas for the whole house and the house of pre-med students next door. When I had joked about the bounce to my mother, apparently she'd secretly sent another check into the registrar without telling me. What would Freud say about that?

Sisyphus had been cursed to roll a boulder up a hill for all eternity for his hubris, and now Boulder was literally rolling down on me. I'd spent the first part of my undergrad

3

at the University of Colorado in the Greek system there— the token nerd in the coolest frat. Perhaps I was Pinto in *Animal House* without the losing of his virginity to the Mayor's daughter on the fifty- yard line scene of the film. The beautiful people of Boulder sometimes made me feel like a pledge and not a full-fledged active member of their fraternity. People told me that I looked like Clark Kent, however when I took my glasses off, I still looked like Clark Kent.

When I had transferred out of CU to Cornell, it was escaping the underworld and reaching the Acropolis. In both Homer's *Iliad* and *Odyssey*, one of the key themes was fate. The Greeks imagined three old women spinning the fates of mortals on a loom. Could fate be changed or was your path in life pre-determined? Was my return to Boulder already spun?

Life on the fate list, excuse me the *wait* list, continued over the next two months as undergrad wound down. I hadn't heard anything from the other law schools when graduation came in June, but I didn't despair. As commencement chairperson at Cornell, I carried the senior class flag along with my Penelope. The absolutely perfect moment of my young life was when we entered a stadium filled with thirty thousand cheering parents. At that moment, that perfect moment, they were all cheering for me.

As I received my diploma, a Bachelor of Science in Urban and Regional Studies, I wasn't just a conquering hero at that moment, Achilles without the heel. I was Zeus on Mount Olympus. Well, if I wasn't on Mount Olympus itself, at least I was nearby— what an ancient Athenian real estate agent might call Mount Olympus *Adjacent*. I controlled my own destiny and could laugh at those pesky Fates and their loom.

Ulysses and his crew had been tempted by the Sirens, over the summer my sirens stopped singing for me, one by one. North Carolina rejected me first, then Georgetown, then Northwestern and finally just days before school began, Duke declined. I would never learn to spell Coach K's last name.

My Penelope wrote me a Dear Ulysses letter when I didn't officially didn't get into Duke that last week of August. Penelope had turned into Circe the witch. Ulysses had won his Penelope back with his archery skills of course, but I was all out of arrows.

The end of summer, I visited my parents, and then left Albuquerque drove up I-25 north with a great deal of sadness, Pinto would be a pledge all over again. I passed Algadones, Santa Fe, Pecos, Romeroville and the aptly named Wagon Mound, then a spot on the map with the improbable name of Levy, New Mexico. There was indeed a giant rock formation shaped like a wagon mound in Wagon Mound, but in the dusty one horse town of Levy, I doubted that there was actually anyone named Levy. When reaching the ten thousand foot summit of Raton Pass between two mountains I crossed between Scylla and Charybdis, two monsters that would eat me alive if I turned back. 444 miles up the interstate from home, I hit downtown Denver and saw those gleaming sixty story buildings. At least with a CU law degree, I'd end up on one of the high floors, preferably in that big building that looked like a giant cash register, right?

Just past Denver, I made the turn onto the most confusing interchange ever, managed to get on US 36 after three tries and headed northwest to Boulder. Once past the city and county of Broomfield, I saw the Flatirons once again. These giant rock formations emerging from a mountain really did look like the irons of the Gods—Hera could use them on Zeus's toga to get out the wrinkles. My sadness went away instantly. They didn't have flatirons in Michigan that was for sure. Perhaps Boulder wasn't the worst place in the world after all. Pinto could become part of this fraternity after all.

We started classes and we had our first brushes with the Socratic Method. Socrates had grilled Plato and Aristotle on geometry, drama and the metaphor of the cave. In our present day cave, it was much harder, even ordinary words had different meanings. Our professors asked us about "consideration" in contracts, duty in torts and transferred intent in criminal law. The words didn't seem to mean what we thought we did.

"Yes," I replied to one professor after a complicated hypothetical the first day of class.

"Can you give a shorter and better answer?" he asked.

"Uh, no?"

He nodded. I resisted asking for a Coors Light with a Hemlock chaser after my first rounds with Socrates and the gang.

Within a few days, my classmates and I were able to compete in this unfamiliar arena. They were as smart as my friends at Cornell without seeming to be as competitive. The key word was "seem" of course. People played ultimate Frisbee and listened to the Grateful Dead, but could remember all twenty-three exceptions to the hearsay rule as well as the rule against perpetuities all while skiing the bumps at Arapahoe Basin.

I enjoyed classes first semester and somehow managed to do pretty well. I remember thinking, if only I hadn't blown the final in Criminal Law, I would have made Dean's List. I figured there'd be plenty of chances in the semesters to follow, right?

If I ever had an Ivy League edge, it was quickly blown away by the Chinook winds that spring, second semester. Civil Procedure stopped being civil. Navigating the rules became a Cretan labyrinth with the Minotaur of Rule 11 sanctions lurking around every corner. Criminals running from the law soon became covenants running with the land as the first semester Criminal Law case became second semester Property class. My Contracts class professor must have put a contract out on me because I couldn't remember the difference between reliance and restitution in the final exam.

After three semesters, halfway through school, my grades were like the Greek islands ... all over the map, ranging from a 65 to an 89. For the 89, I hadn't bought the book, while for the 65 for State and Local Government I had studied my tail off and joined a study group, which made a perfect outline.

Can you say arbitrary and capricious? Seriously. Apparently, I had forgotten to use those magic words "arbitrary" and "capricious" on the State and Local Government exam and that alone had cost me ten points and I had the lowest grade in the whole class. Yes, my major in Cornell was essentially in the same topic as the class, making the grade hurt even worse. In a school where they curved to a 78, my 76 average stranded me in the bottom half of the class.

Luckily, I wasn't Cyclops with my single eye focused on schoolwork, I was more like Argus with a million eyes and they were looking in all directions. Second year, I did mock trial and was on the school's team as one of the witnesses. We lost to South Dakota in the semifinals. North Dakota I could understand, but South? I started writing for the *Colorado Advocate*, the law school newspaper my second year and end up as Editor in Chief in my third.

When I was editor, a great story fell into our laps—a professor failed to make tenure and some students claimed bias. There was even an hour-long takeover of the Dean's office by some student activists. As Editor in Chief, we ran with the story and put it on the cover of our final issue. When the issue was submitted to the American Bar Association contest, they selected the story as second best in the whole nation, and the *Colorado Advocate* was third overall in our class.

In that final issue of the *Advocate*, I wrote "A Third Year Looks Back," which I consider the first real published Jonathan Miller story. When the issue came out, I stood in front of the entrance to the old Fleming Hall and handed out copies to all who entered here. *Extra ! Extra! Read all about it!*

A woman in our class had played the Marilyn Monroe character in a university performance of Arthur Miller's *After the Fall*. She looked like a brunette Marilyn with less makeup and a slightly better head for the logic games portion of the LSAT exam. When the actress eagerly took the issue from my hands she asked, "Is there an article about me in there?"

"Do you want there to be?" I replied.

She smiled a Hollywood smile. Talk about thunderbolts. I had met a muse, at least for the moment. I didn't know it at the time, but my literary career began in earnest.

(I found "A Third Year Back" buried in a trunk all those years later. It sucked. I had my paralegal type it and then I started to edit it to turn it into this story you are reading now. All that remains of the original are the words "sulfur and brimstone slush.")

As an undergrad, I'd been on a quest to find my identity in graduate schools; in law school the quest was for employment. I sent out thousands of resumes but once mixed up a firm in New York City with a firm with a similar name in Anchorage, Alaska. The Anchorage firm wasn't that impressed that I wanted to go into mergers and acquisitions. I don't know what the New York firm thought about my interest in whaling rights.

I must have looked good on paper, because many firms did want to interview me. I flew out to Hollywood for an entertainment firm. The interviewer looked like something out of central casting. Get us a good-looking fatherly type to play the lawyer whose daughter runs off with the skinhead drummer. This three hundred-attorney firm wouldn't validate my twenty-dollar parking tab.

Entertainment law apparently wasn't very entertaining.

I even interviewed with the CIA when they came to CU. I didn't want to be James Bond; I wanted to be James Bond's barrister at three hundred pounds an hour. I advanced far along in the application process and even flew out to Langley, (well technically Langley *adjacent*), but failed the lie detector test when they asked me who I was. I still didn't know. The rejection letter congratulated me on my outstanding academic achievement, just like Stanford.

I hoped to set myself up with a summer associate position and actually did get a call from an Aspen law firm, but they couldn't make me a firm offer in time, so I took a sure thing, a summer job with the largest firm in Las Cruces, New Mexico. That's a decision I think about even to this day.

Boulder grew on me over my three years of school. I even beat Sisyphus; I made it to the summit after all, literally. The spring semester of my final year, I skied until May, reading Rules of Evidence flash cards on the Palavicini chairlift at A-Basin. You can't do that in Ann Arbor or in Palo Alto.

I didn't make Dean's List, but I did pass all of my courses in the end and would graduate on time. Unlike Ithaca, there were no answers waiting for me my final days in Boulder. I'd be one of the fifty percent of the students graduating without a job. As Bono had sung, I still hadn't found what I was looking for.

When I graduated that June, no one had been formally selected to carry the law school's banner so, when no one made a move, I grabbed it and carried the law school banner into the arena. It just seemed fated.

A few weeks later, I left Boulder forever and headed down the interstate to take the New Mexico Bar Exam, just to have a bar under my belt. When I passed the bar, I planned to see where the fates would take me. New York, Washington DC, Chicago, Hollywood, even Albuquerque ... who knew where I would end up? Ulysses' odyssey had ended in Ithaca where he found his Penelope after all those years. My odyssey through law and love had only just begun, and I certainly didn't know who would be there to welcome me when I finally landed.

ARE YOU HAPPY?

At the University of Colorado Law School, my resume opened a lot of doors; my GPA quickly closed them. For that reason, I interviewed all over the country—San Francisco, LA, and Washington—but door after door slammed in my face. Each rejection somehow made me want the next opportunity that much more. In the spring of my final year, I received a letter from an international law firm in New York City. For a twenty-five year old awash in anxiety, this was my last best chance to make it to the big time.

My dad had grudgingly lent me the money to fly into New York so I felt even more pressure taking the elevator up to the top floor of a magnificent old building. The firm's reception area had a tasteful Asian décor; it looked like a firm that did mergers and acquisitions for Samurai. There were beautiful window frames, but the view only went out to the building across the street. The secretary told me the partner would be right with me. She let me peruse the *Wall Street Journal* as I waited. Reading the *Wall Street Journal* while on Wall Street itself—I had finally arrived.

After an anxious hour, the hiring partner ushered me into his office. He was a dour man in his late forties, and had a stack of half-opened files on his desk. Each stack was meticulously separated by yellow, blue and pink post-it notes.

"We don't get many people from Arizona who want to work here," he said with a slight sniffle, barely looking up.

"No, I'm from New Mexico. I went to law school in Colorado."

"I see."

"Tell me about what you guys do here."

Had I really used the word "guys" to describe these masters of the universe? My innocence made him smile; I was clearly not the barracuda lawyer to be who usually sat across from him. He smiled a real smile as he began his favorite part of the interview.

I quickly grew mesmerized by the international litigation the firm handled. The size of the deals, the reputations of the participants, the travel, the excitement, and of course the money staggered me. His war story covered the near calamity of crossed cultural signals in a Tokyo deposition. I almost told him of my only international experience—searching for a drunken buddy in Juarez, Mexico who had gone to the wrong bar and then hitched a cab ride up to Las Cruces.

After about twenty minutes of tales of Rotterdam, Kuala Lumpur and those bums over at Baker and McKenzie, he glanced back at yellow post-it notes on his desk. His world tugged him back.

I needed to say something. Something innocuous, that would keep him smiling, and keep me in this magic place.

"Anything else?" he asked, picking up the yellow file.

"One more, an easy one," I said. Imagining myself as a great lawyer, I wanted a question that I thought I knew the answer to. "Are you happy?"

For some reason that question hit him like a ton of bricks. He actually sank in his seat, stunned. "No one's ever asked me that before."

He avoided my eyes and turned instead to the pile of documents and files on his desk. He made a few attempts to talk, but thought better of it each time. He glanced over at the door, and at the window, as if his cohorts might listen in to some attorney-client privileged information.

Finally, satisfied that the coast was clear, he spoke in hushed tones about his crushing workload, the trans-Pacific travel playing hell with his immune system, and how he somehow wanted something else. He didn't say what, almost as if he'd forgotten.

He was especially distraught today. An impending merger might cost him his job. Then as I sat there in amazed silence, he told me about his divorce and how much he missed seeing his children grow up. He stopped exactly fifty minutes later, as if a light had flashed indicating the end of therapy. He shrugged his shoulders. "I guess the answer to your question would be no."

There was a buzz at the door, and his secretary rushed in. His 4:30 was waiting outside. He nodded to her and then nodded to me. It was time to go. I noticed that he was filling out a form marked "INTERVIEW WITH CANDIDATE ____"

I'll always remember the last words he said to me on the way out "By the way, what were your grades again?"

(NM Young Lawyers Newsletter, Barrister, Coloradan, Denver Bar Association Docket)

I had graduated from the University of Colorado Law School right before I turned twenty-six. I did not have a single job offer at graduation. I decided to take the New Mexico bar, because if you scored in the top ten percent you would be admitted in both states.

In the first week in October, I passed the New Mexico Bar with a few points to spare, but didn't score enough to waive into Colorado. The very next day after taking the New Mexico Attorney's Oath, I moved to Washington D.C. Unfortunately I was unemployed for my first eight months. About six months in, I wrote my first professional article, "I Fought the Law and the Law Won. " It was published in the *Washington City Paper* in April, the next year.

I FOUGHT THE LAW AND THE LAW WON

The old joke says that a hundred lawyers at the bottom of the sea would be a "good start." Well a hundred lawyers would barely start a ripple in a reflecting pool in Washington. Barristers crawl from every nook and cranny in this town, with branch offices in the smaller nooks and outlying crannies. Each year hundreds of zealous law school graduates storm the capital with crisp suits and immaculate resumes, seeking work with a prestigious Washington law firm like Arnold and Porter.

There is no place at Arnold & Porter for underachievers. I take that back, Arnold & Porter does have a place for underachievers. It's a waiting list with over a thousand names. I'm number 997.

My sin was graduating in the bottom half of my University of Colorado Law School class, making me something of a leper among aspiring lawyers, especially in Washington. I chose law school for the same reasons many of my classmates did: I had a murky conviction that in my hands, the law could be a real tool to effect change. And I also hoped that a law degree would guarantee my success in life, or at least a job.

I was wrong.

Three years earlier, I had graduated from Cornell and had made Dean's list one semester. I had no idea where to begin my life, but parental pressure made law school seem like a suitable launch pad. Besides, my score on the national Law School Admission Test (LSAT) suggested I'd be a damn fine lawyer, in the top 95th percentile even.

The University of Colorado, once described by the *New York Times* as a school with "a lingering image of a semi-serious university," didn't carry a lot of clout in Washington. Still, it had a solid grounding in environmental law, and any school that's less than a day's drive from the slopes of Vail can't be all bad.

After graduation from CU, the low altitude of Washington seemed like the land of infinite legal opportunity. At least I felt that way after completing the Marine Corp marathon in less than three and a half hours. Cities like Albuquerque and Denver have only so many places to work. Washington was the way out for me, or so I thought—hundreds of firms, swarms of congressmen, and countless trade associations all supposedly looking for me. I didn't expect a marathon job search. Before I arrived, I mailed eighty well-researched cover letters to the capital city's highest and mightiest firms and waited for the phone to start ringing.

I waited a long time. In some respects, I'm still waiting for that phone call. Pride wounded but soul intact, I went after the smaller, less renowned D.C. firms, only to find that they were also tough to break into. They only hired the underachievers from American University with good summer clerkships. Alas, I had only worked in Pueblo, Colorado and Las Cruces, New Mexico for my law school summers. Las Cruces was only sixty miles from the site of the first atom bomb test. I had hoped that gave my resume some special kind of glow.

It didn't.

I had a few promising interviews at first, but once the subject turned to grades and rank, they quickly resembled a nasty Senate subcommittee hearing.

Speaking of the Senate, I've tried Capitol Hill as well, but it was next to impossible for an outsider to find a job there other than as an unpaid intern. For some reason, the prospect of interning left a bad taste in my mouth. My Capitol Hill interviews were remarkably brief, violating the laws of physics. One 10:00 A.M interview actually took negative time. For the first time ever, I got on the orange line right as the train hit the Virginia Square station and miraculously arrived at Capitol South and in the office at 9:35. After some quick questions about experiences and aspirations I was out the door by 9:39 when I was pushed out by farmers from the district, holding what seemed to be manure samples. When I returned home, at exactly 9:59, I was scared I'd run into myself running out the door to leave in the first place.

One stop away on the orange line from Capitol South was Federal Triangle. My career barely got off the train, much less on track; it might have been the Bermuda Triangle stop. The Federal government seemed the ideal place for an underachiever, just look at some of the people behind the counter at the Post Office. Unfortunately, the line to get hired was just as slow and the background checks were intrusive. Did I really have to put down everything I did in high school?

To sustain my endless job search I took out several small loans, and played the supplicant with parents. After bouncing a check for a phone bill for $39.95, I reluctantly joined the minions who toil in D.C.'s second economy— temporary work. One recruiter asked if I was up for "heavy, heavy phone work," which sounded more suitable for a longshoreman than a lawyer. I tried to keep a brave face at cocktail parties when saying what I did. In small talk, stapling became "metal-paper interfacing," data-entry became "multi-digit computer programming" and of course using the copy machine became the cutting edge field of "repetitive reproductive studies."

My road from the LSAT to *Loser* was paved with good intentions. Yet I somehow knew that I would emerge from the muck and somehow make it big in Washington.

I was wrong, of course.

(*Washington City Paper*)

LETTERS TO LETTERS

Read the classified ads lately? Employers must be embarrassed to use their names in classified ads and hide behind letters and numbers. That is puzzling to me—they should be happy that business is so good that they need to hire somebody new. On the other hand when applicants apply for jobs, they don't have that luxury. Unlike personal ads, lawyers can't call themselves something like "Sensitive Overachiever looking for love." It's embarrassing because every blind submission is an admission that a candidate is willing to work for someone they don't even know.

In the *New Mexico Bar Bulletin*, legal employers often mask their identities behind letters. "Two year associate wanted, experience in bankruptcy and litigation; Write to Box S;" For some reason, I've rarely seen a box "q," "r," and never a box "x."

Which brings us to the cover letter—every job seeker knows to enclose a cover letter with each resume. It shows that the job seeker is genuinely interested in this particular job and not firing them off at random. A good cover letter should display an understanding of the firm's practice as well as convey the job seeker's unique qualifications to fill that niche.

But how do you draft a cover letter to a letter? The following is one attempt.

BOX S
ALBUQUERQUE, NM 87125

Dear S,

I am seeking the Solicitor situation shown in the State Bar Bulletin. I am aware of your sterling status among the letters; in fact the most sizeable volume of the World Book Series is Volume S. Many scintillating and successful words begin with S, although regrettably I am currently S free.

I am also impressed with your strength at the end of words. Many words would not be able to become plural, and would remain singular if it was not for S.

Appropriately enough, I am looking to practice in the field of name changes. My slogan would be "Your first vowel is free, consonants assessed according to law." Obviously I would love the opportunity to tell my clients that if they are going to change their names, S will always be there.

Incidentally, I understand your firm has a good softball team. I can help you there, as I lettered in college.

SSSincerely,
J

I've seen ads in other publications with numbers. "Excellent opportunities for personal injury practice: contact Box 12345."
But what about letters to box numbers? They have far less personalities than letters. How can the job seeker impress good old Box 289 for example?¶

BOX 289
Albuquerque, NM 87102

Dear 289,

I am responding to your ad in the Federal Jobs Register. I have worked for three years for Box 17, which I especially enjoy as it is a prime number. However that does have its drawback, in that my work has not been divisible by others. As 289 is the square of 17, I believe that I would have much to offer, and could bring in potential clients from referrals from Boxes 34, 51 and 68. I would also like to expand your practice to affluent areas like 90210. In law school in the 303 area code, I was 123rd in my class. As the editor of the "NUMEROLOGICAL LAW JOURNAL," I had an article published on "1983 Suits since 1991; too much 12(b) 6?" I am also interested in Title Nine work, although I've done considerable work on First Amendment cases. Please contact me at 505-555-5555.

Sincerely,
505-555-5555

The future of job seeking promises to be even more impersonal with the advent of computers and e-mail. Resumes are already stored electronically, and potential employers can hit a few keystrokes and find their match. Hit {ctrl f5, alt f6} to hire their new litigator. So job seekers might as well be original and write cover letters like the ones above—if not they'll be just another number.

P.S. There really was a "Box S" of course. I sent them a perfectly normal letter. I didn't get the job.

(Barrister, New Mexico Young Lawyer, New Hampshire Lawyer)

I finally did get my dream job in Washington at the Department of Interior, but I wasn't allowed to write anything without the consent of my supervisor, so I went silent for a while. I was learning about the lucrative field of energy and natural resources law. My goal was to be the good guy for the bad guys. I hoped to someday land a job in the private sector where I would tell the evil corporations to respect the environment, all at a decent salary with stock options

Unfortunately, budget cuts forced me out right before I vested. I worked for Congress for a few weeks, and then my mother told me about a job in suburban Chicago with an urban planning firm. It looked like I was leaving the law only a year into my career ...

PLANNING PROFESSION COMPARES NEXT TO LAW

"You're not a lawyer, you're a planner!" the angry voice of my supervisor shouted as I put down the phone. "Don't ever tell our clients that you're a lawyer again!"

A few months before, such an admonition would not have bothered me. In fact, it would have led to a long awaited sigh of relief. Despite receiving a certificate of commendation in my first job as a government lawyer, I had wondered if law was really my life's calling. I turned down the next legal position to become a city and regional planner for a prestigious consulting firm. I would finally be liberated from all the bondage associated with the legal profession, laughing at my law school colleagues as they stewarded cases, proofread contracts, and billed enough to pay for the budget deficit.

I would be free—or so I thought.

Intellectually, my job as a planner would be like a starship captain. I would seek out new civilizations and issue prime directives that would affect people far into the next century. To boldly go and all that.

In my situation in suburban Chicago, I was turned into a dust cube before the first commercial. The planning profession, known for its commitment to people and innovative approaches to protecting open space, does not have the same commitment to its own work place.

The following is not an indictment of the planning profession, nor of my former employers. Rather it is my own somewhat tongue-in-cheek plea of nolo contendere to the crime of unrealistic expectations. Because of the experience I received, this was one crime that did eventually pay.

I couldn't unlearn my entire mode of thinking taught by Socrates and his cronies at law school. Supposedly a legal education is a good preparation for any endeavor.

Much the same can be said about marathon running. If you have the discipline to focus all your mental and physical energy to the twenty-six miles, the theory postulates that you can transfer that edge to the rest of your life. This was clearly not true with my Constitutional Law exam, for example. Its only similarities to a marathon were that they both took the same amount of time and I smelled just as bad at the end.

In writing a comprehensive city plan, I found why my legal background made me uncomfortable as a planner. A plan makes grand pronouncements and sweeping declarations. A planner often boldly states "yes." Yes, you can put a park here; yes, you can prevent a homeowner from building his house too big. A lawyer doesn't like to reply "yes" so quickly; he prefers a shorter and better answer – "no." I kept looking over my shoulder to see if Professor Kingsfield was rearranging the facts to form a bizarre hypothetical.

In planning, I also had to learn a whole new vocabulary. For instance "infrastructure" is not some incurable nineteenth century disease.

One of the appeals of planning is that planners work with the tangible. You can count how many stores there are in a community, how many apartments in a complex. You can even count how many trees in a subdivision, their type, and how many of their leaves will fall.

I did every single damn one of them.

Another aspect of my job involved using architectural drafting tools. This was problematic since my last foray into architecture was my college project, which had long streaks of blood from an accident involving the intersection of cardboard, flesh, and an exacto knife.

Back then the critical reaction could be summed up as "pay more attention to scale, details, and cleanliness." Today, blood on cardboard would be considered "art."

I tried to reawaken these long lost artistic talents when drawing a map of communities surrounding our client's proposed subdivision. Again, given the unintended but definitely creative interpretation of scale, shading and texture, the resulting map would also be considered "art." Unfortunately my map would be banned in Cincinnati for obscenity.

My technical prowess also extended into such complex technical fields as short burst radiation programming and metal paper interfacing, otherwise known as copying and stapling. In planning firms there is less of a division of labor than in law firms – everybody has to do a little bit of everything. Somehow when there are architectural and geographic displays involved, even the most mundane tasks can become beyond the reach of someone with a doctoral degree like myself. You've heard of "Don't drink and drive," a corollary should be "Don't think and staple." Schools should also require at least twenty hours of safety courses before a lawyer is allowed to use an exacto knife.

All the intense pressure was still there. Planners still work hard and bill long nights and early mornings. They also have to deal with billing codes that have five different three digit numbers for the task "planning," none of which you're supposed to use when you're doing something you would normally consider to actually be planning. There is still the fear that you have just advised your client to build a one hundred story building in a fault zone. Finally, planning firms are just as concerned with the bottom line as any ruthless, balding lawyer on TV.

In fact, since planners bill at lower rates than lawyers, there was the added pressure of cutting costs even deeper. Calling information for a phone number, using big tabs instead of little ones, chewing on pens – all were strictly verboten.

Financial constraints also restricted choice of wardrobe. One of the most useful tools for planners in protecting against sprawling suburbanization is the green belt; to a planner it is also something to go with a gray suit.

Finally, there was math. I hate math. Calculating site volume ratio, building volume ratio and opacity ratios under two or three formulas is not fun. One noted political columnist speculated that the current Mideast buildup is in retaliation to the Babylonian's invention of calculus and algebra. Both can be more troublesome than poison gas any day.

It was thus a combination of factors, especially the math part that caused me to begin to realize I missed being a lawyer. I had the shared experience of passing the bar exam, which was admission into an exclusive secret society. Knowing the rule against perpetuities was knowing the secret handshake. There is camaraderie among lawyers missing among other professions that don't force novitiates to endure unspeakable deprivations. Maybe it is because no one else can stand them, but lawyers like hanging out with other lawyers. (In fact, I used to play pick-up basketball only with lawyers, but when it comes to going for the rebound, most lawyers move as if carrying around the entire *Corpus Juris Secundum* on their shoulders.)

There is also an adrenaline inherent in the law. I felt it when I was working on cases helping disadvantaged Indians or battered women, protecting natural resources or fighting for a client I really liked. I also found that I enjoyed humbling a particularly obnoxious opponent.

This exhilaration can be the hidden fun of being a lawyer. In some respects the practice of law has the same secret appeal of professional wrestling, without the tacky jewel-encrusted belts (excluding the few lawyer-planners dealing with green belts, of course). Those who argue that lawyers lack charisma have obviously not seen a certain attorney's television commercials.

So I'm back to being a lawyer, back home in New Mexico, and wiser for the experience. I have more realistic expectations about being an attorney and I'm comfortable with putting Esq. after my name when I write a check to Domino's. I realize that what I didn't like about law is essentially what I don't like about life. I guess stress, disappointments, and boredom will follow me wherever I go. There is no escape. Yet if you can become comfortable with who you are and what you do, you can begin appreciating the tremendous opportunities within the legal profession. There is much about the practice of law that is good, much like the practice of life. Sometimes you have to take a working vacation from it to appreciate it.

Besides, when was the last time you heard a good planner joke?

New Mexico Lawyer

After waking up in DC in January and Chicago in April, I left the Chicago planning firm, but not by choice. I spent a few more months of the fall underemployed back home in Albuquerque. That winter, I finally landed a job at the Public Defender's Office in Roswell, New Mexico when I was twenty-eight. Yes, that Roswell. I felt like I was the one being abducted and taken away to a faraway world.

I would soon learn one major difference between representing cities and representing criminals—cities don't have mothers that call all the time.

After it was clear that I would be spending the next eighteen months in Roswell, I made a vow that I would make the best of it. With God as my witness I was going to get a novel published!!!

On December 26, I started the drive down to Roswell. I brought a tape recorder with me and spoke the following words into it. "This is not the book I want to write ..."

As I passed at the rest stop on the edge of town, I saw a sign that said "Watch for Rattlesnakes" and thus the idea for the Rattlesnake Lawyer was born. Every day, I spoke my observations into a tape recorder, and every week I tried to turn my real life into some semblance of a story.

Roswell was not all bad. While I was down there I met what I thought was the perfect woman. Gradually she became a part of the book as well. There was a line in the manuscript about her. "What's this red beating thing in the trash? Oh I'm sorry, it's my heart."

I honestly don't know whether I said those words first or wrote them in the manuscript. Perhaps because of its honesty, I had an agent for the project within a few weeks. By the end of my first year in Roswell, Rattlesnake Lawyer was optioned by Viacom as a potential television series while it was still just a forty page outline. I was still in Roswell at the time.

DATE WITH A DEFENDER

"You don't fit my expectation of a Roswell public defender," said my date between mouths full of wonton soup at Roswell's best Chinese restaurant.

"What did you expect a public defender from here to look like?"

"I don't know—a cowboy riding a flying saucer, holding the scales of justice."

"Well I've only been a Roswell public defender for a month. Give me some time."

Amanda had attended my high school up in Albuquerque and then matriculated from an elite university. She'd just started her first job as a rookie reporter at the local TV station. Far prettier than Princess Leia, she looked more like Natalie Portman's Queen Amidala from the *Star Wars* prequels. Like Amidala, she wore a touch too much make-up from her hours on camera earlier in the day.

To use the obvious metaphor, we were both aliens in Roswell in more ways than one. At this early stage of our lives here, Roswell felt more like a cross between West Texas and the less fashionable sections of Tattooine, Luke's home world in *Star Wars*. We'd just found each other after many years, neighbors at the one apartment complex geared toward young people in town. Our complex felt more like a bunker in a residential neighborhood of Tatooine's Mos Eisely barrio without the alien cantina for nightlife. Now at dinner, her darting eyes made her seem even more nervous than me, a war correspondent on her first trip abroad, waiting for the rocket's red glare to finally start.

She smiled when she recognized me, when we had passed by the empty pool earlier in the day, and eagerly agreed to dinner. I wasn't sure whether we were really on a date, or she was interviewing me for deep background on the next big story whenever it came.

"When did you decide to you wanted to do criminal law?" Amanda asked, checking off a question on her mental interview list.

"I didn't plan for this, that's for sure. When I graduated from law school, I didn't want to be a trial lawyer, I wanted to save the world. I first worked for the Department of Interior in DC, a research drone on natural resources issues. When I finally saw a case we'd worked on, my supervisor took me to the wrong courthouse. We arrived at the right room just in time to watch a US Attorney use my paragraphs to triumph in an oil and gas royalty dispute."

"I wanted to be a lawyer like that," I said. "A real lawyer."

"That was like something my dad would say. My dad was in the Navy, but he rode a desk. He always said that the Marines always thanked the Navy for taking them to the fight. He secretly wanted to be a marine."

"Exactly, I wanted to be in the trenches, the courtroom trenches. I wanted to get dirty."

"You're getting dirty all right. And Roswell? How on earth did you end up in Roswell? The *Sunday New York Times* arrives on Tuesdays here."

"I keep ending west." I talked about my misadventures in the East and Central Time Zones. "I'm sure I'll end up in California someday."

"Been there, done that." Apparently her internship in Hollywood didn't work out and she was heading east. We both had ended up home in New Mexico like two ships colliding in the night. "Couldn't you get a job at home up in Albuquerque?"

"I'm here by choice. Sort of. When I wound up back at New Mexico, the only entry level jobs listed in the *Bar Bulletin* were for Fifth Judicial District, which included Roswell. They actually paid better than the Albuquerque jobs, especially when you factored in cost of living."

"But why not a DA job?"

I told her about my interview at the District Attorney's office. They had blue blazers with "Fighting Fifth" engraved on the lapel. They wore them for docket call days, but sometimes wore them just for show. Mr. Fighting Fifth actually began our meeting by saying, "I am now going to ask you questions that are off the record and will not be used at all in the interview process." He proceeded to ask me my age, marital status, political party, alcohol use, and what I liked to do on Sundays. Whatever I said was wrong, especially the Sundays part since I didn't repeatedly use the word "church." When he asked about my grades, I almost didn't provide an answer until I realized we had made it to the official part of the interview, and he was taking notes.

Down the street to interview at the public defender's office, I must have crossed over Checkpoint Charlie into the free world. This was also about fighting, but more about self-defense, like legal *ju-jitsu*. Mr. Miyagi, the mentor in the *Karate Kid*, would be proud that we would only use our skills in self-defense. I just felt more comfortable, especially when I met one of my bosses, Pete. Pete boasted that they did more trials in the Fifth than anywhere in the state and even received combat pay. I could be a real lawyer at last.

Amanda laughed when I mentioned combat pay. "I

deserve combat pay," she said. Apparently being a rookie journalist in Roswell did not pay network wages, which explained why she was in the same apartment complex that I was in. "What did you do on your first day as a public defender?"

"I went to jail."

"You go to jail? You don't look like you've ever spent any time in jail. Did you go all by yourself?

"Well, not the first time." I had accompanied a female attorney who was eleven months pregnant. Yes, eleven months pregnant, and her belly nearly took over the cramped interview room of the Chaves County Detention Center. I watched her interact with her client, a man facing the eight year habitual offender enhancement. They both casually referred to the enhancement as the eight year *bitch*. I was terrified that getting bitched referred to something to defense lawyers if they got locked inside.

(*Author's note: Years later, I would encounter the attorney and her son at an event. I was able to casually say to the young man, "We were in jail together once."*)

"Were you still scared when you had to go by yourself?"

"I forgot to close the door and left the jail door open. I figured it would close automatically. I was wrong. If someone had run out they'd be in Panama by now."

"Did you like being locked in? I don't know if I could take it."

"I was breathing heavily after only five minutes stuck in the room between the hallway and the jail pod. Within five minutes I understood why the people in jail wanted to get the hell out."

Our main course came. I wondered if we had ordered Chinese food or Klingon cuisine. This was Roswell after all, so I couldn't really tell whether the meat was of this world.

Amanda didn't bother to eat. "How long before they trusted you with a real live hearing?"

"About a week." I told her about my first solo hearing, a detention hearing for an alleged fifteen-year-old burglar. Unlike the massive Federal courthouse in DC, we had the hearing in a converted broom closet in the old courthouse. It was before a "special master," an elderly woman retired from the school district. The special master did not wear a robe, while I was dressed like the Devil's Advocate's junior associate in a black Ralph Lauren suit with a blood red Jerry Garcia tie. My client sported an Oakland Raiders shirt with matching Raiders tattoos on his neck.

I went on for twenty-minutes extolling the attributes of my poor client who had stolen a video of the film *Scarface* from a convenience store. I acted like the lawyer I'd seen in Federal court on the million dollar natural resources case, citing case law and everything. The prosecutor said nine words total. "He was on probation when this happened, your honor."

Needless to say my client was held in detention.

Amanda smiled. Maybe this was a date and not an interview after all. She touched my hand warmly, but before I could relax, she instantly shifted into full *Sixty Minutes* gotcha mode. "How can you defend someone you know is guilty?"

I thought back to something Pete had said during my interview. He was one of the first people inside the Santa Fe prison after the riots and claimed to have seen the mangled bodies and severed heads. "After you've seen what I've seen, you know you don't want someone going to prison unless their guilt can be proved beyond a reasonable doubt."

I got preachy to Amanda and told her how proof beyond a reasonable doubt, BARD became my mantra by my third day. I almost had it tattooed on the space between my thumb and forefinger much like my clients had the three dots signifying *mi vida loca*. The Constitution, specifically the Bill of Rights, could be tattooed on the palm of my hand as a cheat sheet. It applied to everyone equally. Justice wore a blindfold for a reason.

"Are you saying justice isn't blind down here?"

I kept preaching. During my first month in the Fifth District, I saw our clients routinely overcharged—attempted murder, eighteen years at eighty five percent good time when unnecessary roughness, fifteen-yards-loss of down— would have been the appropriate sentence.

(*Author's note: I haven't been to the Fighting Fifth in years, and would assume that it much better today.*)

She nodded perhaps sensing a two part exposé. "Do you like your clients?"

"Actually, I do; especially the juveniles, because I still see hope." I talked about realizing how lucky I was and how many advantages I had growing up. These kids didn't have SAT tutors, much less stable home environments. Some of these kids never had a chance. I rattled off some statistics that I had read in a criminal defense magazine.

Perhaps my preachiness bothered her. She frowned, changed the subject. "Have you even won any trials yet?"

I was sheepish. "I've only been there a few weeks. I was only handling juvenile cases and misdemeanors. In my first DWI trials, the defendant might have been intoxicated in court, could *sitting* while intoxicated be a crime. As a driver he couldn't maintain his lane, as a defendant he had trouble maintaining his balance. The jury came back in less than two minutes with a guilty verdict. "

"That must have hurt."

"He told me, 'I want a real lawyer and not a public pretender.'"

"Didn't he know that you are a real lawyer?"

I looked down. I had wanted to tell my client I wasn't pretending. This was all too real for me. I was doing my best and not always winning. I learned to take pride in providing zealous representation against overwhelming odds. I did more court appearances in that first month than my former boss at Department of Interior had done in his lifetime.

"So you lose all the time?"

"I finally won something last week. It was only another detention hearing and managed to get a fifteen-year-old shoplifter out of jail, at least pending his trial. I was so happy that I personally took a certified copy of the release order to the jail window. I felt like Moses, I had let my people go."

Amanda laughed at that silly joke. "You don't look like Moses," she said. "And that's a good thing."

"Wait till my second month," I said. "I'm aging rapidly."

When our waitress came by and took away our still full plates, I told Amanda about how the waitress at one of the local Mexican restaurants was dating one of my clients. I never knew how much to tip the significant others of criminals. Should I tip the girlfriends of aggravated batterers more than murderers?

We stared at the empty table for a few moments. We were both still hungry, and not just for food. Amanda asked me if I had any other interesting stories.

"I don't have much yet, but I have a feeling I can get a book out of this place."

"I'd love to read it," she said. "Just don't put me in it."

We walked out into the crisp night. The sky was incredibly clear and with some mysterious objects moving parallel to the spine of the Milky Way. Were they airplanes, meteors, or perhaps unidentified moving objects checking out the scene?

I walked her to her front door of our complex. "I am interested in learning more about what you do," she said, shaking my hand, but implying that a kiss might not be out of the question on our next close encounter. "Let's do this again."

"If you want to hear the real stories, you should talk to my boss, Pete."

She shut the door. I was alone under the stars. I took a deep breath of the clean air. Perhaps Roswell would work out after all. I looked up at the Milky Way one more time, and saw another friendly unidentified flying object. The sky was the limit in more ways than one. It was Roswell after all.

There was a second date, but not a third. Amanda and I never quite worked out. She did have dinner with Pete, and breakfast too perhaps, but that's another story for another time. Speaking of stories, I did get a book out of this place.

I had an agent for the book project within a few weeks. By the end of my first year in Roswell, *Rattlesnake Lawyer* was optioned by Viacom as a potential television series while it was still just a forty page outline. I was still in Roswell at the time.

The manuscript was not to be published as an actual novel for a long while yet. Unfortunately, writing a novel while working as a public defender created a lot of friction. In February, I was told that they were going to review the book. If I violated a single client confidence, I would not only be fired, I would be disbarred. Well, I hadn't violated anything, but it sure was a scary week waiting. I was only fired.

You can read a fictionalized version of my adventures in Roswell in *Rattlesnake Lawyer*.

All in all, I lasted eighteen months in Roswell. On my thirtieth birthday, I then returned to my hometown and worked part time for my mother's law firm as I tried to start my own criminal law practice.

LAWYER IN THE WOMB

When I left the Roswell public defender's department on my thirtieth birthday, my first job was a return to the womb, literally. I worked for my mommy's law firm. My dad owned the building, so the three of us were all together, one big happy family. To make things even happier, I moved back to their home in the high desert foothills above Albuquerque, as I tried to save enough cash for a security deposit for my own apartment in the city down below.

Most of the time, I worked on my juvenile criminal cases from a conflict public defender contract, but my mother promised me that she'd eventually trust me with her big time civil cases when she felt I was ready. I had a handful of juvenile burglary cases at the time, and the prospect of paying clients, especially paying clients old enough to shave, certainly appealed to me.

One day, my parents were heading away for a long weekend, Bora Bora, someplace like that. They'd be totally out of touch. I'd be home alone, and more importantly, "office alone," for the first time. Not only was I supposed to water the plants, my dad stressed that the most important duty was to call my grandmother each and every day. She had helped out the family during some hard times, and they were eternally grateful. My dad still called her every day and now he wanted me to do the same.

They left on Thursday night. The client's meeting with Federal investigators was scheduled for Friday morning. That first night, I rented the movie *Risky Business*, but unlike Tom Cruise, I did not dance alone in my underwear after my parents made it safely to the airport.

Friday morning, I borrowed one of my dad's ties for the meeting. I nearly spilled milk on it as I munched on my Lucky Charms before heading out. The meeting was at the client's sprawling adobe ranch complex in rural New Mexico. The issue had something to do with a few missed payments to some Federal agency. How hard could this be? Inside, I encountered two Federal officials—Good cop, bad cop. "Good" was a bureaucrat in a brown suit, yellow shirt and a red striped tie. "Bad" looked like a professional wrestler with a shaved head. He called himself some kind of an "agent," but didn't give his name, much less his agency. The meeting started slowly. Good took control and asked about incidents on this date and that. My clients cooperated, but Good still wanted just a little more detail here and there. He was friendly about it, used the word "visit," as in "Let's visit about this date right here ..."

"Let's visit about September again," he said, after an hour, still smiling.

Bad abruptly excused himself to go to the bathroom as if September was some kind of code between them. Good's leisurely questioning continued down the calendar—visiting about November, December and especially those twenty eight or twenty nine days of February?

I didn't want to let my mom down, but it was her case after all. I knew I was supposed to object to things, but the requests seemed innocuous enough. I was distracted by some commotion outside—sirens or something.

Bad came back in and nodded. My clients looked over at me, a little perturbed. I had missed objecting to one of Good's visits, and they hadn't liked it.

"Asked and answered," I said, offering some support.

"We'll let a judge decide that," Bad said.

Outside sirens grew closer and closer. Suddenly Bad rose again and headed toward the door. "I have to go to the bathroom again," he said, strangely.

Moments later, Bad returned with more agents, state cops and even some overweight locals from the sub-station down the street. I didn't know that small town cops could have such big time guns. I felt like Tony Montana in *Scarface*, without having any little friends covering my back.

Something snapped in me. It was time to stand up for myself. Not Tom Cruise as the mischievous rich kid in *Risky Business*, but Tom Cruise as the young military lawyer in *A Few Good Men*.

"Let me see that," I demanded and grabbed it away. I looked over the warrant, it was valid. Or was it? Upon closer examination, I saw that the warrant was based on hearsay testimony of a disgruntled employee.

"This will never hold up in court," I said, defiantly.

"We'll see," Good said. "We'll see."

Those were Good's last words of the day, visiting hour was over. Bad was in charge now. He sat my clients down in the chairs, as he sat in the desk. "Let's start with your real names," he said. "For the record."

"Aren't you forgetting something?" I said to him before he could get much past the spelling of their middle initials. I tried to stare him down.

Embarrassed, he reluctantly read them their rights. I looked at my clients. "Take the fifth, " I said. "Don't say a word!"

The clients listened to me. Even more amazing, Bad listened to me. He stopped cold.

Outside, two local cops surrounded the janitor's rickety flatbed truck and nearly defied gravity as they leaned over the windshield to look inside. The janitor looked over at me. "You're the lawyer, right?"

"You can't do that," I shouted at the two very big men. "Your warrant doesn't cover the truck!"

I was bluffing, yet they stopped in mid-air and returned to earth as if I'd said some magic word. Damn, the constitution is a wonderful thing!

Inside the agents seized a few crates of records, but they left. I immediately called a famed appellate lawyer and started on the issues to get this thing kicked. It would take a year, but they would be totally vindicated and even get some money in a law suit. My clients told me two words that I never heard in my years of being a public defender—Thank and you.

I felt like I was a real lawyer for the first time. Hell, I felt like a grown-up for the first time. I couldn't wait until I told my parents. They'd be so proud.

I celebrated all weekend. I told everyone about how I stared down armed Federal agents with only the constitution to back me up. I think by the twentieth telling, I'd fought off the entire 101st airborne.

My parents came home that Monday. They were furious! Huh? I was a little surprised. I had watered the plants, mostly; I had only left one pair of underwear on the stairs. I was about to tell them about my adventure, but they wouldn't hear any of it.

"You didn't call your grandmother!"

And that's when I realized you can be the greatest lawyer in the world, but you aren't truly a man, my son, unless you call your grandmother.

ROUND ONE

If my first trial as a private lawyer had been a prize fight, they would have stopped it. Well, actually a judge stopped it on a technical knockout. Unfortunately, I was the one on the canvas.

I represented a fourteen- year- old accused of a felony. His parents were college professors, foreign ones, and this was their first lesson in the American juvenile justice system. They paid me three- hundred dollars up front, pledged to give me three hundred dollars at the end of the case. They didn't say they expected me to win the case for the final three hundred. They didn't have to.

They said he was a "good boy." When I was his age, my parents were disappointed in me for not making honor roll. In their eyes, Jimmy couldn't have been a criminal—it was all because of fatigue, stress and some unstated "issues."

As a rookie private lawyer, I actually thought that I could win a felony trial on the "good boy with issues" defense without the benefit of an expert witness. I felt that the other three hundred dollars was already in my pocket.

I nearly threw up before the trial began. When I was a public defender, my clients had said that they wanted a real lawyer, not a "public pretender or a public surrender." Was I a real lawyer now that someone was actually paying me for my hard earned services? Somehow I felt like I was an escort, albeit one in lower heels. As I looked around the courtroom at the other private attorneys going before the judge, I realized that if I was an escort, three hundred dollars didn't buy all that much.

The judge mangled my client's name, so I corrected him. This was not a judge who liked to be corrected. He glared at me.

I sat silent for a moment, and then said, "Ready for trial."

"Are you sure?" he asked. "Any preliminary motions?"

I had none. The Prosecutor called an officer to the stand. The officer, 6'5" with a blond crew-cut, looked like a Nazi storm trooper, but I noticed that his six year old son sat in the gallery. The son was drawing pictures of his daddy on the stand.

Daddy waved to him. Both the judge and the children's court attorney waved to him as well.

That couldn't be good.

The officer did not testify about "issues," but talked about evidence instead—physical evidence, scientific evidence, and most importantly eyewitness evidence, his own. The boy's mother looked at me. She'd taught molecular something or other, and wasn't that comfortable with life out from under the microscope.

"Why does that cop get to keep talking about fingerprints?" she asked.

"The State has to prove their case beyond a reasonable doubt." I said.

"But when are they going to talk about what was going through Jimmy's head?"

I didn't know what to say. When I got up to cross-examine the cop, his son stared at me. "Please don't be mean to my daddy," he said.

I shrugged.

The kid wouldn't stop staring at me. "Any chance a reasonable man in an impaired condition, might have been confused and not realized that he was doing a crime?"

"Nope."

"Are you sure?"

"Yes."

The cop came down, gave his son a hug, and then triumphantly left the courtroom, holding the picture in his hand.

Another cop repeated the first cop's testimony, word for word for word, right down to the "nope" response to my blistering "are you sure" cross-examination. He also had a child waiting out in the gallery, who looked identical to the first. This one played with a toy dump truck, and went "vroom, vroom."

The children's court attorney rested after that. I made a motion for a directed verdict and the Judge nearly broke out laughing. The little boy kept vrooming.

The judge called a recess, and muttered something about, "Why don't you guys see if you can work something out. I will find him guilty and you don't want that."

Out in the hallway, the boy's mother told me how unhappy she was with my performance. I hadn't laid a glove on either cop.

"You're the worst lawyer ever," she said. She looked like she was about to hit me herself.

A guard tapped on my shoulder before I could respond. "The judge needs to see you." Saved by the bell.

Inside his office, the judge told me I'd better plead the case before I put the boy on the stand. If I pled, the boy would get six months' probation. If not, it was real time.

I then had to go back out into the hallway, in front of the officers, and explain the situation to the parents. "You're giving up on us." The mother said. "We paid you to win."

"Well, I can't win."

"Mom, dad," the boy piped in. "Maybe he's right."

After a few more minutes of pleading, they reluctantly agreed.

"If we had a better lawyer," his mother said under her breath.

We followed the guards into the judge's chambers. He literally laid down the law. The mother asked if Jimmy could still go skating at the local rink. The judge glared at her.

Of all the items on his probation agreement—the drug tests, the curfew, the reporting it was the skating that was nearly the deal-breaker.

"Mom, I don't have to go skating," the boy said at last. "I'd rather play video games at home anyways."

"Let's talk outside," the mother said. I got up to follow them out.

"Alone," the mother said.

After an anxious meeting outside in the lobby, where we heard a snippet here and there about skating versus video, the family returned. They said nothing further as Jimmy turned to the judge. "I'm going to plea."

We went to court for the plea. Even though I knew the verdict, I felt like an anxious fighter waiting for the decision. I somehow mumbled through my part.

The judge paused as I finished. He looked at all of us, like Darth Vader without a hood, about to change his mind and unleash the Death Star

The mother looked at me "But you said …"

I would soon learn that the three worst words a lawyer could hear from a client were "but," "you," and "said."

"Your honor, I thought we had an understanding." I tried to at least pretend to rise for the final bell. "We're ready to go back to trial."

The judge smiled. Maybe he took pity on me, or maybe he just dreaded my direct examination even more. "I'll accept the plea." he said at last. "Six months of probation."

Before I could finish my sigh of relief the parents and their son were already out the door. I knew that if I even thought about the other three hundred bucks, I'd get hit with a disciplinary complaint.

I sat in a bench in the gallery on the verge of tears. The father was right. I was the worst lawyer in the world. If only I'd studied harder in law school and got a job at a big firm.

I felt a tap on my shoulder. I was surprised that the boy came back over to me as his parents waited in the parking lot.

"Thank you," he said.

"For what?" I replied. "I lost."

"Yeah, but you cared. No one else really does. You're doing what's best for me." He smiled. "And besides, right now, they're so mad at you, they forgot to be mad at me."

He shook my hand, and then hurried back out.

When he violated again in a few weeks, the parents got the best lawyer money could buy. The boy stayed out of jail. The "good boy with issues" defense worked, at least in sentencing.

On his third offense, the boy was indeed sent up. This time for good.

I saw the parents in the courtroom that last time as they walked away with their lawyer. They didn't say anything.

I then went up to court, begged the judge for leniency for a drunk driver who said that someone must have slipped a "Mickey" into her drink. She smiled at me. I found myself believing her in spite of myself.

Somewhere a bell rang. A new round had begun.

DEATH AND DIALING

Many young lawyers have represented first degree murderers. Many young lawyers have had to take second jobs, like telemarketing, to make ends meet.

Am I the only one to try to do both at the same time?

As I began my solo legal career in the basement of my father's insurance office, I had no advertising, no referrals and not even my name anywhere on his building. All I had was a public defender "conflict contract" to get five fannies a month onto my single plastic chair. If two people did a crime, the Public Defender's Office would get one defendant and I would get the other. The Public Defender's office had first choice. Think about that one for a moment.

The luck of the draw handed me the most brutal case of my life, all for a flat fee of $150.00 plus seven percent gross receipts tax. A few years before, a young man was convicted of murder. I was doing the "motion to reconsider."

I'd always liked to fight the good fight, or at least get the fight reconsidered, but $150.00 for what often was one hundred fifty hours of work was ridiculous. I was going down for the count. When my car broke down at the exact moment that my credit cards maxed out, I needed some quick cash for a new clutch.

There was a telemarketing firm right next to my office. One day I talked with the owner as I finished doing my business in the men's room. I said I was always looking for new opportunities. Before I could even wash my hands I had a job offer. Thankfully, he was out the door before we could shake on it. Why couldn't my legal interviews be this quick?

His offer involved working afternoons. Since all of my court hearings, including the alleged murderer's, were in the early morning, I could be a lawyer in the morning and a telemarketer in the afternoon.

When I was a bratty ten year old, who thought I'd be the greatest writer and/or lawyer in the world, I'd told my dad, a successful insurance executive, that I'd rather "eat barf," than sell insurance like him. When I told him my situation at our Sunday dinner, he told me to get used to my new diet.

On Monday, I questioned witnesses all afternoon in an attempted murder case. I felt like a successful attorney and hoped I wouldn't have to go through with telemarketing. But on Tuesday morning, I fell off the beam while balancing my checkbook. My dad was out of town that day, so I didn't have a car.

So at high noon on a hot and gusty spring, I walked down the long dark flight of stairs and reported for duty. The telemarketing office was in deep in the nether reaches of the complex, like a secret military bunker designed to survive a massive terrorist attack. I settled into my cubicle, hooked myself into a mass of wires. I strained the limits of the cords to look around at the other telemarketers. Voices did not match appearance. One sounded like Burl Ives in the *Rudolf the Red Nosed Reindeer,* his deep, mellifluous voice set to break into a rousing Christmas song at any minute. In real life, he looked like an anorexic elf on amphetamines.

The supervisor informed me of the company's client for the week—a law enforcement organization lobbying to keep criminals in prison.

I took a deep breath as the supervisor pressed a button for us to begin. I felt like a science experiment. The computer suddenly announced that it was "now dialing." Suddenly a phone number came up on the screen, and a female voice said "hello,"

What was I supposed to say now?

"Hello?" the female voice repeated.

I pressed a key and the computer flashed a script in a soft green glow. I introduced myself then scrolled down each highlighted line. With each objection, I hit another key and had a response. Unfortunately, the voice suddenly said "good bye."

Before I could take a deep breath, the computer noted that it was "now dialing" again. Moments later a new voice, male this time, said "What the hell do you want?"

The computer monitored the time, amount of calls, the amount of money raised, and whether people were slightly rude or really rude. That category was called "Irate remove." Thank God, the computer didn't measure my heart beat, or sweat glands.

I was "irately removed" the first few times out, as I mechanically plowed through the script. I warmed up to it after a while and quickly made a few sales. Some of the people I talked with were extremely friendly. One seventy year old woman told me that I had a sexy voice and pledged twenty dollars.

As I questioned people about crime on my calls, I listened to some extreme views. The people I'd never want on a jury were the most likely to contribute. A man who wanted to hang 'em all pledged a hundred. There were retired people who had rabid views on crime, but lacked the means to contribute. I was tempted to do the hard sell with that group. "If you don't contribute at least twenty-five dollars, I know a lawyer who will get a murderer back on the street."

We'd have a twelve minute break after every seventy-three minutes. At 1:13, on my second day, I rushed next door to my office, to find not one, but two fugitive situations. One of my female shoplifting clients had picked that exact moment to turn herself in and her warrant hearing was scheduled right for the middle of my shift. Luckily I twisted a friend's arm to handle it for me, offering the vague excuse of having to "make some real important calls." I then had the remaining six minutes to convince an aggravated batterer to turn himself in after three months as a fugitive. He wouldn't turn himself in, but he wouldn't hang up either and droned on about his tale. At 1:24, I did an irate remove on him.

Back in the bunker a few minutes later, the computer rang up someone who sounded nervous when I mentioned that I was calling to raise support for law enforcement. No, it wasn't my fugitive again, but it might as well have been. This person thought that since I was somehow connected, however vaguely, with law enforcement I'd have to turn him in. "You'll never get me alive!" he said, hanging up on me before I could finish my pitch about how he could "help fight crime."

After a week, the telemarketing money wasn't quite as good as expected. My car's clutch was almost in my grasp, but I wouldn't make enough from telemarketing to afford psychotherapy to recover. Like flying, there had been hours of boredom spiced up with a few minutes of terror. The computer had rung up an ex-girlfriend, who was now working for a big time law firm making the big time bucks. When I heard that voice again, I almost threw up, didn't leave a message.

Meanwhile, I used every ounce of energy preparing for

the reconsideration hearing. Unfortunately the hearing switched from the morning to the afternoon, so I'd have to take a day off. When I told my supervisor he gave me an ultimatum. If I took the hours off I'd lose my index and be bumped down into lower pay scale. I had no choice. I couldn't exactly tell a judge that I was late for court because I was on the phone.

The big hearing took place on the second Wednesday of my telemarketing ordeal. As I walked up to the podium, and the judge stared at me, I would have given anything to be back in a safe room, connected to a computer that automatically dialed and gave me answers to every objection.

By the time I made my closing argument I started to roll. Although my voice was a little ragged, I kept plugging away as if there was indeed a computer inside me as my companion. I talked about how my client had met the challenges while he was incarcerated, and had proven himself capable of becoming a productive member of society.

Make no mistake I believed every word I said.

The next morning, I went back to court. The judge told me that his hands were tied because of the severity of the crime. I then had to talk to my client and tell him the news. That afternoon I went into the bunker and hooked myself up for three more shifts of seventy-three minutes straight of dialing. I had the best day of my career. At 1:14 p.m., I found out about Anna, a potentially big client. I quickly called them back and set up the interview in the morning for the next week. Anna told me that I had a good phone voice.

Two weeks later, the clutch paid for, Anna referred some more people to me. One potential client wanted to give me her credit card number over the phone to pay for her retainer. "Anna was right. Your voice is cool."

So to all you complaining lawyers, there are much worse ways to earn a living.

I talked with one of my contacts in Hollywood. I told him that I had a great idea—A lawyer telemarketing to pay the bills. He told me that it wasn't believable.

(*Barrister*)

JERK RELEASE

The best job interview I ever had was in the work release facility of a local Detention Center. While he was waiting for his trial on grand theft auto, my client, "Joey," was eligible for work release. I had been hired by his beautiful girlfriend to get him out of jail. She looked like one of those Disney teen stars who had gone bad. Even though Joey had two or three, or possibly four felonies (if you counted the ones from Texas); she would stick with him through eternity. The woman I had dated last week didn't return my phone call after I asked her to help out with the tip after an expensive dinner at Scalo's.

I sat with Joey in the blank meeting room of the old work release facility as he showed me the paperwork. He didn't have a job lined up yet, and had only four hours to gain lawful employment, before they transferred him to the west side facility for the next six months.

"They'll kill me over there." He mentioned something vague about a rival gang. "You gotta help me, man."

He looked at me with big brown eyes, like a tattooed puppy dog. The work release facility was bad enough, a sort of purgatory for those waiting to be judged for their sins, so west side must indeed be hell. I felt for him. After all, I had spent six months on the wait list for Georgetown Law School and never made it in.

I also had self-interest at heart. My tough negotiating skills had led me to agree to a two hundred dollar retainer, and his mother was supposed to pay one hundred dollars with every paycheck. His mother subsequently checked herself into a mental hospital, so her contribution was now unlikely at best. Considering that most lawyers in this town charged ten grand or more for a simple felony, I was about to check in to the ward beside her.

Joey claimed to have a good lead on a job at the stockyard. Well, he didn't know how good it was, but it was his only lead at the moment. He didn't have the points for phone privileges yet, so I would have to make the call right there in the sprawling Work Release Common Room. It was crowded with inmates at midday—if it was a bus station, all buses must have been delayed for the next six months.

After a few rings, a gruff voice answered the phone. "Who the hell is this?"

I didn't say I was a lawyer, just that I was "making a call for Joey."

"Yeah?" The employer said gruffly. "I can barely hear you."

Reception was indeed terrible beneath all the concrete and razor wire. The other inmates must also have been causing static and interference. Their stench alone would be enough to mess with the radio waves.

"Hey, you guys mind?" I asked. "I'm working here."

Joey stepped back a few steps, motioned to his buddies who reluctantly followed.

"Hello?"

The phone was practically down my throat before the employer replied. "You don't have to shout, now what the hell do you want?"

"I'm calling about the job." Joey pointed to an ad. "The one in the newspaper listing."

"Do you have any experience?" The employer asked.

"No, it's not for me" I shouted. "It's for Joey."

"Does he have any experience?"

I had to motion Joey to return. His buddies followed him back until they were surrounding me again.

Joey said something about a couple of summers working with his dad before his dad got sent up.

"Yeah, he has experience," I said. "He worked for a couple of summers."

"References?"

"You got any references?" I asked Joey. He looked around at his fellow inmates. DWI 2nd stood next to Aggravated Burglary stood next to Mr. Domestic Violence. I nearly dropped the phone. "These guys are my homeboys, man."

I tried to be polite. "You got anyone else? "

Joey finally mentioned some friends of his dad. I passed the names along. The employer actually knew a few of them.

I decided to take control of the interview. "His ultimate goal is a permanent job in the stock industry."

The potential employer took a long breath.

In his line of work, people didn't talk about ultimate goals.

Silence. "Well?" Joey asked anxiously. His buddies edged closer to me …

I was saved by a burst of static from the other end.

"What?" I yelled into the phone.

I had to move the phone until I caught a radio wave that must have burst through the window. "Does he have transportation?" the potential employer was asking.

I looked over at Joey. "There's a bus that leaves here every morning at seven AM and picks you up at five."

I sighed. "Yes, he can get there."

"I don't know," the man said. "I don't know."

The inmates grew closer, until I could feel their breath against me. I looked at Joey again with his puppy dog eyes on the edge of tears, even the tattoo of the virgin on his arm seemed to be crying. He really wanted this.

I thought of all the job interviews I'd had, and all the jobs I never got. But at least at the end of the day I didn't have to go back to lockdown.

"I'll vouch for him." I took a long pause. "I'm a lawyer." I gave out my number. I caught myself before adding something. "I'm his lawyer and I can honestly say he really, really wants this job."

"Most lawyers wouldn't do that," he said. "He can start tomorrow. Make sure he brings in the papers from his unit's social worker."

I quickly hung up the phone, amazed. The employer had known all along, that my client had been in jail and still had hired him.

I looked at my client with envy. How many times had I interviewed only to wait a month before getting rejected because I was under qualified, overqualified or a bad fit? Why couldn't I have interviews like this?

As I walked out the door, my feelings of felon envy got worse. The employer hadn't even asked my client about his grades.

Unfortunately, he violated a few days later. The work release facility would eventually close. Still the guy did get his job back, and his girl.

FELON ENVY

At thirty, by light of the day I slowly became a successful lawyer. Unfortunately, by night I was not much of a lover. I had no women in my life and this infuriated my father to no end. Being a criminal lawyer made me feel even worse on this issue, I suffered from felon envy. Some of my clients had a lover in every judicial district while I couldn't even score lunch with the cute Vietnamese clerk at the Civil Division Filing window of Metro Court. Criminal Division Clerks I could understand, but Civil?

As I've often complained to everyone I meet, almost every felon in an orange jump suit has a woman holding up a sign that says "Jimmy, Cellblock B, I love you." No one had ever held up a sign for me.

I told my father the story of one felon who was such the romantic that he repeatedly violated the conditions of his house arrest for liaisons at his partner's house. She was a codefendant, and he couldn't see her. For each violation the felon received four days in jail and was then released.

I'd asked the man why, he gave up his liberty every weekend. He'd smiled, "She's worth it."

I'd indeed met the woman in question at his sentencing. She was worth at least six months, possibly seven in solitary super-max even.

My father shook his head when I finished that story. "You're an ivy-league educated lawyer whose been published in national magazines, he's an uneducated burglar who's been in federal institutions. You shouldn't compare yourself to him."

"But dad ..."

"You should call our friend's daughter Jessica, she's a graduate student."

"I don't know."

"I could always give her number to one of your clients."

I shook my head in rage. And thus began a race, not against time, not against myself, but against the Men of Max Unit in cellblock B.

It took me a while to get up the courage to call Jessica. I felt like I was back in junior high. I finally made the call on a Sunday. I only reached her machine, which said something about being gone for a while.

"Did you call Jessica?" my father asked on Wednesday.

"I did, but she didn't call back, maybe she's on vacation, a long vacation."

"Maybe her machine isn't working," my dad said. "What was the name of that burglar who was here yesterday?"

I waited until Thursday and called again, my tone a little more desperate. In my law practice, I return the phone calls of attempted murderers, aggravated batterers and criminal sexual penetrators. And she's too good to return my call? It had been more than a week and still no call, her "vacation," even a long one, should be long over by now.

A few days later, she finally returned the call. She'd been an exchange student in Australia or something like that. She apologized, and then apologized again. I accepted.

We talked for a few awkward minutes. "How are your classes?" I asked.

"I really don't like them," she said. "Except for statistics."

"Oh." I said. "By the way, I'm trying to switch from law into screenwriting."

"Oh," she replied.

She had to go study, and I had to return a call from some criminal's mother. I didn't bother to set up a date.

"Did you call Jessica?" my father asked the next day.

"Yeah I did, but there really wasn't much chemistry."

"Actually her mother said that she really thought you were interesting. You should take her out to lunch."

I should have said no, but my dad's insistence made Jessica seem like the Holy Grail, well she was the grail next door.

I set sail again that night. "Do you want to have lunch?" I asked her over the phone. "Maybe we can meet on Friday."

"I'm busy this week. Midterms. How about next week?"

I nearly punched myself as I checked my calendar. "I'm busy. I have a trial."

"Well maybe later in the month."

My trial depressed me further. I represented a young man accused of a string of burglaries across the southern part of the state. His alibi involved a different woman on each of the nights. All were prepared to testify. After the Assistant District Attorney (ADA) interviewed the women in the hallway, he actually dismissed the charges against the guy. The cumulative power of love I suppose.

My female clients also did not offer me much moral support. I met with a young trafficker and told her about her options in choosing residential treatment centers. She wasn't paying attention. She whistled at a young man who was being taken over to court by the two deputies.

The young man smiled back warmly. "Who was that?" I asked.

"Just some attempted murderer," she said, as if talking about the captain of the junior varsity. "But he's cute."

After a week more of back-and-forth, which seemed testier than some of my plea negotiations, Jessica and I finally hooked up for a Monday dinner at a Chinese restaurant. The *moo goo gai pan* was spicy, but conversation was bland. My stories and jokes fell flat as a moo goo pancake; I couldn't feign interest in the tribulations of graduate school. After a few more awkward moments over coffee, I knew that this was not the woman of my dreams after all.

We split the check and went our separate ways.

"How was your date?" my father asked me that night, as if asking about the results of a biopsy.

"It was okay, but I don't think it's meant to be."

"I'm really sorry." He was more hurt than I was.

The next week I had to relay a message from a client's girlfriend to him. He was in jail and she wanted to get married before he got sent up to the big house. He wanted to know whether he could get out of prison through holy matrimony. I had to tell him that marriage was not an alternative sentence.

Once I told him I'd be able to get him a furlough for the wedding, he accepted. His girlfriend said she'd wait a few months for him. She would wait forever.

I was still down in the dumps, but then the phone rang. "My name is Mary," a pleasing female voice said. "My mother said I should call you about lunch sometime."

I shook my head. Not again.

Then I got to the next message. "My boyfriend's in trouble," a desperate female voice said. Her smoky tones sounded right out of a film noir. "I want to hire you to help him. I love him so much."

I thought for a second. I called Mary first about that lunch date.

SENTENCING OF A PSYCHIC

"I'm a psychic," Lilith said before I could even begin the client interview in my basement office. "I work for one of those telephone hotlines."

I wasn't a psychic so I glanced down at her paperwork to read her aura. She'd been charged with aggravated battery on her neighbor. Her court date was set for next week in the next county over, a county that was filled with ancient ruins from vanished tribes. She'd come here because the county also didn't have a single lawyer in private practice. Ancient ruins, no lawyers, could that be coincidence?

Lilith wore black of course. In her snakeskin cowboy boots and cow skull jewelry, she looked like she was channeling Georgia O'Keeffe's evil twin. She certainly didn't look like Whoopi Goldberg as the psychic in *Ghost*, gushing "You in danger, girl."

Lilith couldn't sit still, she pulsed with energy. So did I, but I'd just had my third cup of Starbuck's power Frappuccino in a can. Before discussing her case, I asked her a few friendly questions about the occult. Lilith was devout in her beliefs. She muttered something about "being connected to the universe." Ironically, the case was aggravated battery. Lilith had connected her left fist with her neighbor's nose.

"She started it," Lilith stated. "She had a bad aura."

"But couldn't you just will it away?" I asked.

"Some auras have to be adjusted *manually*."

I told Lilith that my great mental powers could guarantee a 180 days suspended sentence, for simple battery and mandatory court costs.

Lilith didn't smile. She sat very still and closed her eyes for a moment. The vein by her temple pulsated for a moment. I felt some vague static electricity. I had this vision of Darth Vader killing one of the Death Star commanders, his mind utilizing the "dark side of the force."

"I hope you're right," she said.

The courthouse was a small brick behind the interstate. The parking lot was unpaved—big muddy lumps and deep puddles. The earth constantly shook from the passing eighteen wheelers or whatever had even more wheels than that. Perhaps this had been the site of an ancient burial ground, and the bodies were pushing their way to the surface like zombies out for an evening snack. I shook my head at the thought, but hurried inside nonetheless.

The inside of the court was no sanctuary. It was a full docket, and people were huddled three deep in the court's small antechamber. The various drunk drivers and possessors of controlled substances had pallor about them as if recently undead.

I had six cases that afternoon, Lilith's was the last. Still in black, she sat in one of the thirteen chairs in the antechamber. "It's going to be awhile," I said.

"An hour and a half," she replied without looking up.

I entered the courtroom and closed the door behind me, and nothing seemed right in the courtroom. I handled the preliminary hearing of a "felon in possession" that didn't go so well. It didn't take much to prove that my client was indeed a felon and did indeed "possess." It was hardly a demonic possession; he actually possessed an old shot gun in his car.

After the guilty verdict, the ADA scurried away before I

could close Lilith's plea bargain. Dejected and empty handed, I checked in on Lilith in the gallery.

Lilith hadn't moved. "Last case didn't go so well," she said. "I can tell."

I looked back at the closed courtroom doors. There was no way she could have known what had happened. "I better find the prosecutor and get you that plea," I said, feeling a sudden note of urgency.

"Is there anything else I can do?" she asked strangely.

Before I could figure out what she meant, the ADA insistently called me back to the courtroom. Inside, the prosecutor wanted to know what we'd do on my second case for the day—a young boy who had stolen a goat. I wondered if the boy's motive was some satanic rite. His heavy metal band t-shirt had a few too many pentagrams for my liking.

"The goat was found on your client's parent's property," the ADA said in a brusque tone as we addressed the judge. "Case closed."

"That's my favorite goat, your honor." The victim, an elderly woman piped in. "She's like part of the family."

The judge was about to bang down the gavel, when suddenly I had a flash of insight, as if someone, or something had planted a vision in my brain.

"There's a gap in the fence," I said, although I'd never been there. "That's how the goat escaped."

The prosecutor wilted, as if I'd pushed her down. "I'll drop it, if the goat's returned" she said in a soft voice.

"Done," I said. "Now about Lilith."

The ADA was already interviewing another cop in another case.

Lilith's case came and the plea was exactly as I had predicted, — simple battery, suspended sentence with mandatory court costs. I saw Lilith's victim in the flesh, a fifty-something small town Sunday school teacher — the kind of woman who wrote multiple letters to the editor about the dangers of Halloween in the public schools.

"I want her to have no contact with me whatsoever," the Sunday school teacher said as the judge asked if there was anything else.

"Any comment to that, Mr. Miller?" the judge asked.

I felt another charge of static electricity and I rose. "You mean physical contact, your honor?"

"Or phone calls," the Sunday school teacher said. "I get hang-up calls in the middle of the night."

Lilith smiled up at me, a sly smile.

"My client won't make any *phone calls* your honor."

After the gavel came down, the Sunday school teacher hurried out into the dusty sky. She did not look back at either of us, almost as if she was scared that she would turn into salt just like in the bible when Lot's wife looked back at Sodom and Gomorrah.

I was momentarily angered, but got over it quickly. "So why do you two really hate each other so much," I asked Lilith as we stopped by the door.

She said nothing, and then stared at me again. The vein by her left temple throbbed.

I felt some static for a moment, then nothing.

She frowned. "For a moment there I thought you had the gift."

"I can predict a jury verdict fairly well," I said with a smile. "Usually that's because my client is guilty."

"Try again," she said. "Concentrate."

I closed my eyes for a moment, and tried to see something in my head. Nothing … When I opened my eyes, she was gone.

BURGLARY BLUES

I fight for truth, justice, and the aggravated burglar. For the last few months, I've had the "cowboy contract" with the New Mexico Public Defender department. I would get in my white car and ride across the desert to represent offenders in such towns as Truth or Consequences, NM. (Yes, that's the real name of the town, more commonly known as "T or C"). At the completion of each case, I felt like the Lone Ranger as I'd helped a poor burglar through the criminal justice system. Then I'd take off my cowboy boots, change into Nikes, and jog into the sunset.

What I liked best about being the hired gun, was that once the ride home began, the case was over and done. I kept in contact with a few of my clients to be sure, as I helped them through their probation, but I never had to deal with the victims again. That was fine with me. To me victims were like the lynch mob in *Hang 'em High*.

But then my computer was stolen right out of my office and I became a victim myself.

Perhaps my computer was stolen by someone like the burglars I'd represented. Small town burglars tend not to be as proficient in the art of burglary as their big city cousins. If they were, they wouldn't need to be rescued.

Often they weren't very smart. He liked the movie about the Kennedy assassination conspiracy—KFC.

Yet my small town juvenile burglars were my most challenging cases because their lives were on the edge of the steep canyon—some would go on to college, some to corrections. For a fourteen-year-old, going through the system on their first burglary charge is like a law student's summer clerkship. They'd get to try out the life for a while without any real responsibilities or consequences. Unfortunately, many decided they liked the life and tried to make senior partner by the time they're eighteen.

I liked to think that my representation, my commitment to them as people, influenced that decision.

So I used to cringe when talk radio callers would say "criminals have rights, what about the rights of victims?" To me victims were often just another person to cross-examine, after the forensics expert. On direct, they'd claim their mobile home contained the Mona Lisa before it was defiled by my client.

"Excuse me sir," I'd say on cross. "But didn't you say the painting was dogs playing poker on black velvet. Are you still insisting its value is over $1,000,000? Remember you are under oath."

After my own burglary, I now understand that certain things in life are indeed worth a million to you. My machine was on the edge of obsolescence, but as a TV ad had declared, the content of your computer was "you." I wonder if the alleged burglars erased the hard drive. It had all my criminal forms—entry of appearances, motions for discover, demand for jury trial; so once caught they could help out their lawyer. I even had my brief for the New Mexico Supreme Court on the issue of ineffective assistance of counsel, in case their hired gun is shooting blanks.

I can live without my legal prose since I've always fashioned myself more of a writer than a lawyer. Somebody has to write "Plaintiffs reincorporate each and every allegation contained in the general allegations of the complaint, as if set forth in full," and it might as well be you.

But those silicon pathways also held a bit of my soul—an unfinished novel, a sold but un-produced screenplay, and ideas for TV movies never saved on disk. All lost forever.

Or were they? The sheriff suggested that the computer might have been shipped out and resold in LA so who knows. Perhaps some UCLA student, who bought a computer cheap, no questions asked, is on the cellular right now with some concept for a new TV series—*T or C PD Blue* or perhaps *NCIS T or C.*

So will I still zealously represent burglars? Of course. They have a constitutional right to a fair trial and I will still try my best to get them equal justice under the law. I will still believe that there is hope and somehow I can make a difference in their lives.

I won't always ride so quickly into the sunset.

(ABA Journal, NM Young Lawyer, East Mountain Independent)

At thirty-one, I grew tired of the life of a struggling solo lawyer. I needed a break from law. *Rattlesnake Lawyer* had been finished and was still under option, so I hoped to nudge the project a little further down the line. My dad cosigned for a loan and I decided to take a break from the practice and I enrolled in a ten week class at UCLA-Extension.

BETTE MIDLER SWEEPS MY FREEWAY!

During the summer after my second year in law school, I worked in the dusty, desert town of Las Cruces, New Mexico. One 105 degree Saturday, I put aside the books to go to the only cool dark place in town—the movie theater. The movie was terrible; I should have stayed in the office and kept on reading the "cram-down provisions" of the bankruptcy code. When I looked up at the screen and saw the "written by" credit, one thought flashed into my mind—I could "written by" better than that.

A few years of practicing law later, I would finally have my chance.

The time to gamble was fast slipping away. At thirty-one, I was ecstatic to still get carded at a local pub, but that happened less and less with every weekend. When I scheduled a meeting with a client at the Bernalillo County District Courthouse, I told her to look for a lawyer that looked really young.

She was in her twenties, but married to a convicted felon and already had three kids from three fathers. "You don't look that young," she said.

I went home, checked my calendar. I had already filled my quota of public defender contract cases for the year and wouldn't get my next case on the new contract for a few months. This was my window. I made a call to UCLA-Extension and signed up for their ten week program for spring quarter. I would take classes in Screenwriting and Comedy writing. I now had ten weeks to become a star, or at least write clever dialogue for one.

Why did I do it? The idea of going out to LA was not totally farfetched. One conglomerate had already purchased an option on one of my ideas for a TV show. The show never made it of course. Still, the amount of money I had received would still qualify me for a public defender myself, should I switch to a career of crime. I looked at the ten weeks as my summer clerkship in the film industry.

When I finally arrived in LA, I had a place to stay already set up. I moved into an apartment complex right by Universal studios which I'd found with a few phone calls back in New Mexico. "Celebrities live here," the leasing agent had told me over the phone, and I used that as a rationalization for the exorbitant rent, twice what I'd paid in Albuquerque. The first night in the complex I met a guy who had a recurring role on *Baywatch* as "guy on beach."

The next morning, I had my first real "Hollywood moment" in front of Warner Brothers Studios eating at the most popular Mexican restaurant in the world—Taco Bell. Two guys sat next to me, eating double-beef burrito supremes and practicing their pitch to the networks. After listening to them intently for a few minutes, I offered them some advice. "Give the show more of an edge," I said. "Make the main character more likeable. By the way could I get some of your taco sauce?"

They ignored me. Probably just as well.

My first week, I had to clear up one loose end back home. As I killed time in the Beverly Center while waiting for a meeting, I had to telephonically approve a motion for a burglar's furlough to see his new baby. Next to me, a model was on the phone with her agent, yelling in a French accent how she wanted to be in Paris next week, not Milan.

72

I was loudly insisting the furlough was for forty-eight hours not twenty-four, and that the sheriffs' office would transport him from the joint to his home.

"Some people don't understand what I'm going through," the model said to me as we hung up at the same time.

I didn't know how to respond.

My first official "taking a meeting" took place at a renowned agent's home/office in what had once been described as the slums of Beverly Hills. The agent's assistant greeted me in a dusty living room. He was wearing an expensive suit and tie worthy of court even though he was working in a home. The assistant apologized, told me that his boss had literally talked so much that he'd lost his voice, and conducted all his business from the bedroom. He was not allowed to see anyone, doctor's orders. The assistant would have to act as a go-between.

The assistant shuffled between the rooms a few more times. I felt like he was taking my prayers to God himself. Unfortunately, the answer to my prayers was "no."

In the weeks that followed, my metaphor for LA became the 101 freeway. We've all seen the signs on highways that say "This mile maintained by the Rotary Club." One mile on Highway 101 was maintained by singer/actress Bette Midler. Form the mental picture in your mind—Bette Midler singing *Wind Beneath My Wings*, her orange hair billowing in the exhaust smoke of a thousand cars as she bends over the side of the road to pick up discarded bubblegum. For me, I felt like merely driving on that road made me feel like a movie star.

When I was stuck in traffic at lunch, one of a cast of thousands, spending an hour looking at that damn sign, I felt homesick for the deserted Highway 285 back home.

At UCLA-Extension I quickly realized that I wasn't in Cruces anymore. During my orientation in one class, everyone gave their life stories. My classmates ranged from seasoned studio execs to farm boys, fresh off the boat from Iowa, Indiana or even Australia. But there were sharks out there as well. One guy announced to the teacher, "I'm an agent; I'm just taking this class for exposure."

I was about to say that I had represented someone on exposure charges but thought better of it.

On my second class, I asked out one of my classmates. She worked at the make-up counter at Bloomingdales, but also wanted to "produce and direct." She seemed excited to meet a writer and a lawyer. "What a sexy combination," she said with a smile.

Our date didn't go that well, when she realized I wasn't much of a writer and I wasn't even a lawyer admitted to the California bar, and not very sexy besides. I couldn't further her career either on screen or in court. A few weeks later, I saw her out with the exposed agent.

The pressure and rewards were intense in the program. In one class, we wrote scenes that were performed by actors in the class to put on a "showcase" for industry at the end of the quarter. For my showcase scene, you might remember the film, *Scarface*. In one scene, Al Pacino brandished a pistol in a man's face, yelling "You want some of this?"

The man said, "No."

I was unable to get Al Pacino for my skit, I was however able to cast the guy who didn't want some of this.

I learned about the collaborative process during the final five weeks, putting the scene together and getting it ready for the show. The idea came from a deep personal experience—the woman of my dreams left me for someone utterly different from myself. While working with "the guy who didn't want some of this," my original idea metamorphosed into five minutes about famous French crooner Maurice Chevalier and a moaning dwarf. Really.

There were some Hollywood players in the audience that night of the big showcase. Right before intermission, one of the writers had allegedly signed a three picture deal. I shivered, could magic could strike twice in one night?

Somehow my little skit worked on stage. The "guy who didn't want some of this" was good, but the moaning dwarf was hilarious. Still, I didn't know whether to be happy or not. Were the people laughing with us, or at us? And where was that agent with the three picture deal in his pocket?

When the curtain came down, a man approached me afterwards. I would now get my answer. He dressed in gray. He wasn't an agent after all, but a lawyer with a big firm, who had heard about my legal background from a classmate. Close-enough, I thought to myself.

As I launched into my thirty second pitch about my "transplanted lawyer" story, he smiled intently. I was about to hand him my card, when I noticed that his was already out. I had wanted him to introduce me to the right people. As I looked into his eager eyes, it hit me like a ton of bricks. He thought that *I* was one of those people.

My last week, I had my big lunch with two producers at a nice restaurant in the Valley. The young hot shot and his boss both dressed identically in all black on a hot, windy day. I wore a blue polo shirt.

I ordered something with leeks in it. Lunch lasted two and a half hours as the older producer claimed responsibility for every good idea ever in Hollywood.

"I was the guy who told Cecil B Demille to let Moses part the Red Sea in *The Ten Commandments*," he said in a blissed-out Californian drawl that barely masked his Brooklyn roots. "He was just going to end the movie right there with the Israelites stuck on the beach, if it wasn't for me!"

I couldn't tell if he was joking. This was my last chance, but I couldn't concentrate on the meeting. I had parked in a two-hour space because I was too cheap to spring for the valet. If I was towed, I couldn't afford to pay. The last thing I needed was a car in impound, just as I was about to leave.

I apologized and stood up. They interpreted that as a power play. I must be heading out to the arms of someone else. They panicked. As I headed out, the Mr. Red Sea told me to call him that night. He'd finish the script by then.

My car was still there, two blocks away. That had to be a sign. That night I called Mr. Red Sea at the stroke of seven.

"I read your script, kid," he said. "I've been a producer for twenty years, and your script got me excited about what got me into the business to begin with—story, characters, surprises—you got it kid. After reading, I started writing my own script again, the one I never finished."

Suddenly his phone clicked. "Sorry kid. I got to take this call. I'll get right back to you."

He didn't get back to me that night, nor the next night. He didn't return my five phone calls the next day, nor the night after when I finally had to leave LA and go home. As I write this, years later, he still hasn't gotten back to me.

Someday, I don't know when, but someday—you will sit in a theater on a hot summer afternoon and see my name in the credits and say, "I can write better than that."

(NM Young Lawyer)

AN EXTRA CRISPY INTERVIEW

Number three on my top ten list of worst interviews was with David Letterman's production company in Los Angeles. After receiving a "secret" job list from an inside source, I faxed ten resumes. Within thirty minutes, Letterman's company, Worldwide Pants called. I talked with the current Assistant, reminded him that I was an attorney, just not one in California yet. He sounded pleased and mentioned that my legal abilities "might give me a leg up."

We set an interview for the next day. I wondered if Letterman would be there for the interview, and if so whether he would ask me about my grades.

The next morning, I glanced at the gigantic billboard over Beverly Boulevard, which announced "Television, now in Regular and Extra Crispy" with the gigantic heads of Craig Killborn and David Letterman staring eastward.

(Note, I look back on this many years later, who is Craig Killborn?)

I drove my battered Subaru to Television City, the CBS lot. After a long bit of searching, I parked next to a biggest satellite dishes I had ever seen.

The office was nondescript. Letterman was not there. His Vice President in charge of something or other, dressed very well, but talked faster than any other human being that I have ever met. Perhaps all the electromagnetic radiation had affected her -- like the Star Trek episode, where the bad guys vibrated at a higher frequency than the poor crew of the Enterprise.

She looked down at my resume, scolded me for applying

for an assistant job if I was already an attorney. Apparently she hadn't talked with her Assistant about his choices yet. "Why are you even here?"

I mumbled about "not being admitted in California and looking to learn about the industry," but that didn't satisfy her.

She asked me about my ultimate goal. I mentioned "Development," finding film or television projects -- something open ended.

Whatever I said was wrong. Way wrong.

She scolded me again -- my career options were as different as brain surgery and teaching kindergarten.

Still reeling, I tried to play it safe, asked her about her job. She warmed up a little as she replied that much of it was hiring writers for Letterman, and some of his other comedy and dramatic projects. Then she segued back into how her assistant was someone who she would feel comfortable with.

It was clear from her body language, after only seven minutes (which would probably have taken twenty minutes in normal time) that I was not going to feel comfortable with me.

I thought to myself -- what would David Letterman do? I launched into my comedy writer spiel -- I was a unique voice because of my legal background, yada, yada, yada . . .

It only took a blink of an eye for her to stop the interview right there after the second yada. She lifted up her right hand like a traffic cop, called me "disingenuous," whatever that meant. Apparently, I had broken an unwritten law by interviewing as an assistant to pitch myself as a writer. She walked briskly to the door, opened it.

It took me a few blinks to realize that this was her way of asking me to leave. Speeding up even further, she wished me the best of luck, didn't offer me her hand. I tried to save myself, told her that I was from New Mexico and kind of slow, and still adjusting to LA.

She gave only the slightest bit of encouragement -- *if you want to be a writer, you should "Write, write, and write."* But made it clear that she didn't want me to "write, write, and write" for her, ever.

I walked out slowly from her office, my head held down. The fire from Dave and Craig's gigantic eyes made me feel like I was rotisserie chicken turning on a spit.

When I went home there was a new message from someone else. That interview ultimately would of course, make it to number 1 on the list.

(*AFI Networks Newsletter*)

INTERVIEW WITH MYSELF

My absolute worst Hollywood job interview was at a small production company in the far reaches of NORTH Hollywood. The difference is more than geographical. North Hollywood might as well be North Dakota with better weather. In the Hollywood Reporter the production company advertised the position as "Your big break into Hollywood." Well, I really needed a big break at the time, so I faxed in a resume and was delighted to get an interview. I had seen it all and heard it all already and I hadn't even graduated from Film School.

When I arrived at a cramped space in the valley, they made me wait. The big boss hurried out, and left me with his intern who was in his sophomore year at Cal-State Northridge. The kid looked barely old enough to shave and wore a t-shirt for either a film or a band that I had never heard of. He stared at my resume dumbfounded, or perhaps just dumb.

"Dude, you should be interviewing me," he said after scanning the third line of "experience."

He had a list of scribbled questions from his boss, and it looked like he could barely read the writing either. Considering my luck with interviews lately, interviewing myself didn't sound like such a bad idea.

"OK," I said. "Your first question is why would someone with my qualifications apply for a job like this?"

The kid stared at his scribbled notes. It was like I was a psychic.

"How did you know I was supposed to ask that?"

I shrugged. "The answer to your question is that I want to change careers and I know that you have to start at the bottom."

He smiled.

"Let's see," I said. "Your next question is probably whether I'd be willing to do a lot of menial tasks to learn about the industry. Well, the answer to that is yes. As I said I know I have to start at the bottom."

Good answer.

We spent a few more minutes together, and I hit all of questions, although not necessarily in order.

He said he'd get back to me. Nothing for a week.

I called and left a message. Another week, nothing. I didn't have to be a psychic to know what that meant. Interviewing myself was one thing, but how could I not return my own phone call?

(*AFI Networks Newsletter*)

Hollywood Fright

"He knew right then he was too far from home."
Bob Seeger, "Hollywood Nights."

I had my first real "Hollywood night" in a UCLA Parking Garage. I was auditing an entertainment law class at UCLA. The class was hardly the Continuing Legal Education programs I was used to back home. There were actors, actresses, even a few rockers mixed in with the people in suits who wanted to be their lawyers.

Even in such an eclectic group, Natasha stood out. She dressed in expensive clothes, always in black, with jewelry that you didn't get from being the girl next door.

At first glance I thought she was an actress in one of those unrated thrillers you see that show late night on cable. I thought of the tagline of a forgotten film — she mates ... she kills. In her late twenties, she had the intensity and world weariness of a former child-star gone wrong who had just made her comeback.

She wasn't a Lindsay Lohan of the law as she carried a big briefcase rather than a Gucci purse. I soon found out that she was a lawyer, top in her class from a top law school. She had just left the big firm to go out on her own.

I sat next to her the first night. She was brusque at first, and talked more with an aspiring rocker/rapper on her right. I was jealous as they talked about "A and R," whatever that was. I blurted that I had actually been optioned. She didn't believe me at first, but on the second class I actually brought in the option agreement and showed it to her.

She started paying more attention to me in the weeks that followed. Over the next few lectures about "ancillary rights," we exchanged notes during class like high school kids. She knew her movies and her music, often personally. One of her law school classmates had done the ancillary rights agreements for either Janet or Michael Jackson. I could recite lyrics from songs, and lines from movies. That counted for something at least.

Despite our rapport, I never had a chance to talk with her after class. She always acted like she had someplace more important to be. Still, I persisted. In my early thirties, I had always been the master of my domain, the class clown from elementary school through the bar review class, and now that movies were involved, I was practically the king of comedy. One night, after I had exchanged a particularly witty note, she sat still for a moment at the end of class.

"It takes a lot to make me smile," she said as she looked at me with her deep green eyes, then touched my shoulder with her delicate hands. "But you've succeeded."

She asked me out for a drink and we drove in her car, a black Lexus, as she took me to an unfamiliar bar off Wilshire. Inside, I told her my Roswell stories, and she was fascinated. Every time I told her one of my well-rehearsed tall tales of my crazed clients, her eyes lit up. She laughed at all of my jokes, perhaps laughed too hard for my tastes.

In the smoky light, I saw my ex-girlfriend in Natasha, or perhaps I saw what I wanted my old girlfriend to become. She was circumspect in revealing too much about herself and her practice. She did reveal that she liked to shoot at a local shooting range. She said that she carried a small silver handgun. I wanted to see it, but she demurred.

Ever the storyteller, I of course launched into the story

about how one of my clients had done an armed robbery, but forgot the gun and told everyone to wait for a second while he ran out to the car and got it.

Perhaps she was glad that I had taken the spotlight away from her because she leaned closer to me and whispered in my ear. "You're very talented," she said, and after a pregnant pause. "Let's go."

She grabbed the check away from me, and paid for it with her Platinum Amex card. I looked closely at it; it had a man's name etched across the bottom.

"Who's that?" I asked staring at the card, trying to make out the mysterious surname.

"Don't worry about him," she said, quickly handing the card to the waiter.

I am a criminal lawyer, the words "Don't worry about him," always make me worry about somebody.

We returned to her Lexus and drove back to the UCLA parking garage. It was well past midnight, the garage was dark and empty except for my white Saturn, its yellow New Mexico plates glowing eerily. Confident, I was about to tell her that I'd follow her back. That's when I realized that her car door was locked on my side. My heart's RPM rate increased.

"There's only one more thing left to do," she said.

Instinctively, I tried the door again. Still locked.

She reached into her purse and searched for something. I caught a glimpse of her silver revolver gleaming in the yellow lights of the garage. I heard a clanging sound. Handcuffs?

I fiddled with my seatbelt but it too was jammed. This snake had bitten off more than he could chew. She smiled at me with a dark smile. "Found it," she said.

What the hell had she found?

A million film clichés of the femme fatale raced through my mind—Linda Farentino in *Last Seduction*, Glenn Close with her knife in *Fatal Attraction*, and of course, Sharon Stone with her ice pick in *Basic Instinct*. I even remembered some French actress in the movie *Betty Blue*—a letter opener.

You know you're a struggling screenwriter when other people's movies flash before you in your last instants. She looked at me again in those deep green eyes, then lifted something silver out of her purse and then opened it, and handed me her business card. "I'd like to represent you," she said. "Let's do lunch sometime."

Unfortunately, she finally read the script and didn't like it much. The black widow was going to find another mate, or perhaps another victim .... .

WILD PITCH

I went to a Hollywood pitch meeting as a writer and emerged as a criminal defense attorney. In my pre-Hollywood life, I had counseled over a thousand clients as a lawyer, on charges ranging from first degree murder to trespassing at school. I used the same deep, slow voice for nearly all of them. My clients often suffered from some kind of attention deficit disorder, so I rarely used big words, repeated the key points over and over again, and emphasized the positive as I explained the difference between a deferred and a suspended sentence in the plea agreement.

My "Hollywood pitch voice" was sort of my lawyer voice on speed. Hollywood producers also have attention deficit disorder, so I rarely used big words, repeated key points over and over again and never talked for more than five minutes straight. I just talked much faster and never mentioned anything remotely negative. Again, the ultimate goal was often getting to an agreement, but this time I wanted it to be a "pay or play" as opposed to a lawyer's "pay or plea."

This meeting was at a producer's home on the west side. As I looked for parking, I was happy enough to find something on the street near the three story modern-looking apartment complex. Inside, the home was a collection of artsy artifacts and the producer reminded me a bit of my own mother. She had a nice quality about her in the way that she offered me tea and cookies that would remind anybody of their mother, or perhaps the mother they never had. I swore I could smell last night's apple pie in the air.

The home was immaculate, yet all of the doors were closed. If it had been my home, the dirty laundry would have lurked behind one of those doors, but I figured that all the rooms were probably just as clean as the living room. She seemed that kind of a mom.

The pleasantries over, we started off on a good note. The producer informed me that her assistant had read my legal thriller script and she wanted to hear about all of my other potential projects. I talked about my various experiences as a lawyer and how I wrote about "law and life."

"So you really were a lawyer, then?" She asked. "So do you have any true crime stories?"

"I guess so."

It was time to switch from a curve to a change-up. "As a matter of fact, I based most scripts on my real experiences. For instance when I used to represent juvenile delinquents on murder charges ..."

She stopped me in mid-sentence. "Then you should talk to my son." She paused for a moment. "Not about scripts, but about law."

Before I could regain my balance, she hurried over to one of the closed doors and produced her son. Perhaps she did have dirty laundry after all. On first glance, he was hardly my vision of a juvenile delinquent, but was indeed on probation for various minor charges. Yet the charges were getting progressively worse, and his six months of probation kept getting extended until it now stretched for two years. Some of his friends had been busted on weapons charges, so his mother was justifiably alarmed.

He sat down and was surprisingly polite. He reminded of the nice kid that I represented on the trespassing at school charge, who had graduated to murder. I told the boy my standard stories about staying out of trouble, yet I somehow managed to make them seem both "commercial and edgy." It was weird, but it seemed that I was talking to the son, yet pitching to the mother.

After about twenty minutes of cautionary tales about the juvenile justice system, she stopped the meeting to take her son to therapy, and told me to meet her to continue the meeting. We played the second half of our double-header in a coffee shop as we waited for her son to "talk through his issues" and get his court-ordered urine test. The mother was tense, but she still seemed eager to hear my ideas—both legal and literary. One moment we were talking about "setting something up at Showtime," and then the next we were talking about "alternative sentencing" for her son.

After an hour or two, the boy came back from therapy and apparently had filled the specimen jar with no ill effects. As his mother got up to buy him a Carmel Frappuccino for his troubles, I talked with him some more. Now I was totally in lawyer mode, yet he seemed to want to hear the funny story I had about the criminal who ...

I thought about Samuel Goldwyn's famous quote "if you want to send a message, use Western Union." The fact that the boy was even opening up to someone at all was a good first step. I then told him about the time I met a female killer with my zipper down. He laughed.

His mother returned. It was getting late, so we called the meeting on account of darkness and they went on their way and I went on mine. I felt confident that the boy would be all right, after perhaps a few more detours outside his mother's friendly confines.

I may not have sold a script, but I think I saved a life.

(AFI Networks Newsletter)

I was thirty-two when I returned to New Mexico without getting the big Hollywood break during my first of two sojourns out there. Despite by best efforts at finding a publisher or a producer, *Rattlesnake Lawyer* was still 400 printed pages stuck in a brown Kinko's box.

I renewed my public defender contract, and flittered between legal employers and having my own firm. I hadn't totally gotten California out of my system. You know the line from Hotel California? "You can check out anytime you want, but you can never leave."

I had a variety of work situations in the years that followed. None were permanent. It seemed like one week I had my own practice, the next I worked with my mom, and I even worked with some other attorneys to pay the bills.

SYMPATHY FOR THE DEVIL'S ADVOCATE

At thirty-one, I had pitched myself as a writer to producers in Hollywood. At thirty-two, I sat in a lawyer's conference room in Albuquerque, New Mexico pitching myself as a lawyer to a young man facing twenty years in prison. I'd initially impressed the producers of *The Simpson's* with my ability to remember an episode with a sign reading "I can't believe it's a law firm." As I went through the consequences of the young man's "habitual offender enhancement" and the difference between probation and parole, I decided not to talk about anything animated.

I felt the weight of his stare as he decided whether he would hire me or pass.

How did I get here? The easy answer would be by driving nine hundred miles down Route 66, but the real reason was more complex. I couldn't justify an unpaid life of pitch meetings and porn stars (and pitch meetings with porn stars, but that's another story) without a steady job. The ads in the New Mexico Bar Bulletin called for "Associate Attorney, Please send writing sample." I could hardly send my spec episode of *The Practice*, much less my kick-ass *South Park* spec ("Cartman joins the mob!"). After my tenth rejection letter, I had the horrible realization that a published novel, a Master's degree, and produced television credits would never erase the fact that I didn't make law review.

When I got an offer from the tenth biggest firm in New Mexico, I knew that the closest I would come to Hollywood would be my remote control. I could always pretend that Hollywood was still calling my name when a cinema employee asked, "Do you want butter with your popcorn?"

My first day of my second career as a lawyer did not begin auspiciously. I put up a poster for the movie *The Devil's Advocate*. The caption said "The newest attorney at the world's most powerful law firm has never lost a case, but he's about to lose his soul." The poster died a quicker death than most of Keanu's non-*Matrix* films at the box office. The senior partner made me take it down.

"It's just not professional," he told me.

I wondered if I had sold my soul.

I couldn't wear my Screenwriter uniform of a blazer and a black t-shirt, even on casual Fridays, and it took a while getting used to reading the New Mexico Statutes Annotated or the Uniform Commercial Code. I have read some bad scripts in my time, hell, I've written some worse scripts, but nothing compares with the Uniform Commercial Code in terms of lack of plot and derivative characters.

I liked the fact that murderers were quicker at returning my calls than producers.

I kept calling all my old contacts in LA on the phone. Although, once when my boss came by while I was pitching my "Jewish/Asian romantic comedy with a twist," I had to abruptly launch into my lawyer voice pretending to recite "the tolling of the statute of limitations with the filing of the docketing statement."

After he walked safely by, I quickly switched back to my crystal meth Hollywood voice and finished the pitch. I looked into the eyes of the accused man. In that moment, all the hundreds of rejections in Hollywood passed through my mind—"Not compelling" or its opposite, "too over the top," and of course "somebody's doing something just like it."

He waited another beat, closed his eyes. Dear god, no! Not another pass. I could take it from a film company, but not from a Felon. He opened his eyes, said nothing further. He took a deep breath, and then reached for his checkbook.

"Don't forget to include the gross receipts tax," I said.

(*AFI Networks Newsletter*)

Earring Impaired

I was a lawyer over thirty. If Santa Fe is the "City Different." My home town of Albuquerque should be called "The City Same." I have always been more Albuquerque than Santa Fe. Someone told me that I looked like Clark Kent of *Superman* fame. I laughed.

"Unfortunately, when I duck into phone booths, I still emerge looking like Clark Kent."

A few months ago, I had my ear pierced in an LA mall. I then went to a nine dollar haircut place and uttered the unfortunate words "surprise me" to the barber.

She did.

Someone who cuts hair for nine dollars has a far bigger capacity for surprise than you might think.

I had returned to Albuquerque to be a lawyer all over again. My tail was firmly between my legs. LA had beaten me pretty badly. Still, I hoped that I could let people know that Clark Kent had now become cool.

My legal career as a shaved head attorney with an earring began by sitting in for a friend, defending a deposition in a civil case. I went to downtown Albuquerque to a prominent insurance defense firm, and sat next to my witness.

Nobody said anything.

"I have an earring now," I said to opposing counsel, turned my left side toward him.

"I used to have one during college," he said. "But I let the hole heal up."

"What do you think?" I asked the court reporter, a

middle-aged woman who looked like a bookkeeper for a funeral home. "Could we start now?" she asked. "I'm in a rush."

Two hours of testimony later, I was dreaming of palm trees. I tugged at my ear as if it had some magic power to get me out of here. Why the hell had I come back?

"You're way too young to be having a mid-life crisis" the court reporter said, interrupting my thoughts.

"My mid-life crisis was last month," I told her.

The next week, I went to jail to visit a criminal client, a member of the *ESP Gang*, aka the East Side Pyros or something like that. These guys did not read minds, they busted heads. He had a skull tattooed, five holes in each ear, and a few more on his nose. I didn't even want to know what else he had pierced. Now that he was in jail, all the metal was removed and somehow he looked naked.

I thought we'd have some kind of kinship, now that I had street credibility.

Nope. He was in an even worse mood when he saw my ear.

"Take that damn thing off for court," he said. "They'll think you're a little punk."

He was looking at a couple of years, so he had a right to be worried about being represented by a little punk rather than a lawyer.

"Don't forget," he said ominously.

Unfortunately, I was so busy preparing for court that afternoon, I forgot to take it off as per my client's request.

It didn't matter. In court almost every male lawyer, every cop, every probation officer, even the judge had earrings of their own. The only one without an earring in the entire courtroom was a multiple offender with a skull tattoo on his neck, and he was the only one staring at my ear.

The hearing was successful. I don't think anyone cared about my appearance by the second paragraph of my sentencing plan.

The moral of the story – it's what is in your heart and your mind, and not what's on your ear that matters in law.

I took the damn earring off the next day.

THE FUGITIVE

I am a lawyer in New Mexico. I was also a fugitive from California.

I was still on the lam as I parked in a dirt parking lot next to an abandoned white car and breezed through the metal detector in a courthouse somewhere in New Mexico. Little did the guards know that stashed in my pocket was a crumpled, but active arrest warrant from a small town in California.

Ironically, I was in court to plead my client to a charge of concealing identity. Unlike Harrison Ford in the film of the same name, I wasn't even a very good fugitive. I had left the California authorities with my forwarding address.

My rap sheet wasn't very long or very cinematic. When I lived in LA, I had left town on a Friday afternoon to visit with an old girlfriend up north. LA was a jealous mistress and wouldn't let me leave; traffic on the 101 seemed to stretch all the way to San Jose. As I stared out, utterly impotent, at the belching exhaust of a shiny, silver BMW, every beckoning cliché of the open road raced through my mind. As if it was fate, I switched to a classic rock station and heard a familiar refrain:

Get your motor running,
Head on out the highway,
Headed for adventure,
Or whatever comes my way.

"*Born to be wild*," I sang along with the chorus.

A hundred miles out, the traffic finally thinned and I was in open country at last. It was dark, but I could still make out the outlines of the brown, barren hills. I felt the bounds of civilization loosen just a little as Southern California ended and the Central Coast officially began. A billboard proclaimed a restaurant was "famous for pea soup."

"I hate pea soup," I muttered under my breath.

As if he heard me, a California Highway Patrol squad car edged out onto the road just in front of me. He drove at a constant rate of fifty miles an hour. I had out-of-state license plates, so I slowed and stayed right behind him for a few miles, always careful to stay below the speed limit. I swear that I gave him far more room than the Silver BMW back in LA. Suddenly he pulled off the road and let me pass. I breathed a sigh of relief—too soon.

A moment later his lights whirred and it all began.

"But I wasn't speeding," I protested when he came over.

"No one said you were speeding," he said, handing me a ticket to the tune of a hundred and fifteen dollars. "You were following too close, and that's even more dangerous."

I was a lawyer after all. "I plead not guilty," I said. "Set a court date."

He was polite and efficient and quickly let me back on the road and I didn't think anything more about it. I then moved back to New Mexico.

Two months later, long after I had forgotten my visit to the land of pea soup, I received an official-looking letter.

"Dear Sir/Madam:" it began. "This department has a warrant for your arrest ... This letter does not preclude arrest on warrant at any time." The bail was 340 dollars. Did I mention that I had two hundred dollars in my checking account at the time?

This was the real thing. Given the advent of national computers, I could be thrown in jail anywhere in the country and spend hard time with gangsters and serial killers.

Cool.

I called California immediately. If they wanted me, they'd have to bring me in. Hopefully, the media would be there as I walked defiantly into the jail, as vendors hawked *Free Jonathan Miller* t-shirts while the cameras rolled.

Unfortunately, they wouldn't extradite me, the bastards. They told me my only choices were to fly out there to fight the ticket or pay it and be done with it.

By the time I had finished talking with the California authorities, it was too late to go to the bank to get the check. I had to lay low for a while until the heat died down, or I could still make a break for it. I called a few friends to see if they'd drive around the back streets of America with me, eat frozen burritos at 7-11, and sleep in stolen cars in old trailer parks. They all politely declined.

My mind quickly envisioned a screenplay. Given the recent trend of movies about people on the lam from the law and America's fascination with the dark side, I came up with *Natural Born Tailgaters*. Two messed-up kids travel around the country following other cars too closely. You've heard about the *Fast and the Furious?* How about *The Not Fast Enough and the Following Too Close?*

I couldn't pay the ticket the next morning either, since I was stuck in court on that concealing identity plea. I could hardly ask the judge for a postponement for my client on the legal grounds that I was an outlaw. I scanned the gallery and saw anxious defendants waiting for the law to come down on them. I clenched my fist in solidarity.

As I waited with my client, I glanced at a beautiful, sad-eyed woman with tall proud hair, who strained for glimpses of her boyfriend as he was brought in from the jail.

"Why go for local talent?" I almost said, reaching into my wallet to show her my warrant. "I'm bad. I'm nationwide."

Although no words were said, she looked at me strangely as if she sensed that there was something different about me, something dangerous. She smiled. I nodded at her, then hurried up to the bench as my client's case was called. After we did the plea, I explained to my client the twenty-seven or so conditions of his probation, and the consequences of even the most minor violation.

"One bad urine sample and I'm sending you up," his probation officer had said on the way out. By paragraph seventeen of the probation agreement, a life of crime didn't sound like fun anymore—especially if you got caught.

My client paid me the rest of the money he owed me. I felt a sense of relief. I could finally pay off the debt. Who says crime doesn't pay?

I left court and drove briskly to the bank, excruciatingly careful not to drive too close, purchased a money order and sent it to California, certified mail. Yet, I will always remember, that for a short while I was a wanted man.

(*Barrister*)

ALTERNATIVE ENDING

"Does he love me?" Kim said anxiously to me, as if love could indeed conquer all, or at least get her out of jail without having to report to pre-trial services. We were in the cramped holding cell behind the crowded courtroom. Even in her drab baby-blue jail outfit, Kim's radiant Korean beauty still shone through. What was it with me and Asian women? Unfortunately, time had finally conquered the auburn dye in her long black hair. The barb-wire tattoo on her left arm was also fading fast.

"Hey lawyer, are you listening to me?"

I wasn't. For some reason *déjà vu* had just hit me hard. As my mind search for some long forgotten memory, I couldn't muster a response.

She grabbed my arm. "Will he wait for me for the year? I could get out now and then we take it to trial and win."

Win? That wasn't going to happen. She'd actually been innocent of *most* of her original crimes, but her original lawyer had got her one of those pleas that promised probation but came with a long "tail," a lot of time if she violated. Her falls off the wagon and onto the bottle had brought her back here to a probation violation hearing. She was only a year away from her nursing degree, but now that year would be spent doing straight time in county jail if she was lucky and took the plea to a "technical violation." That lucky year plea offer expired in exactly seven minutes. In the alternative, she could ask for a full hearing. If she won, she could walk away, but she faced eleven long years in prison *when* we lost and the judge counted all the barbs on her wire.

There was a reason that the habitual offender enhancement was called the "bitch."

I was rooting for love of course. If she thought he loved her and would wait the year— six months with day for day good time—everything would work out just fine.

I tried to break the tension as I gently, very, very gently, attempted to remove her arm. "Remember, marriage is not an alternative sentence."

Déjà vu struck me again, this time right in the gut. Where had I heard that lame joke before?

She tightened her grip. "Ask Troy," she said. "I just have to know before I decide. Ask him!"

"Now?"

I didn't need to wait for her response as the tear flowed down from her left eye. I was following a script that had already been written, and it was time for me to exit, stage right.

Stage right took me right through the courtroom's Monday morning docket call, through the middle of the judge doing case number for on the docket, another probation violation sentencing. Trafficking, I think.

That's when it hit me, why I had felt part of a script that had already been written. I'd already written it myself.

On page sixty-three of my manuscript *Rattlesnake Lawyer*, in a chapter called *Alternative Sentence*, a lawyer had proposed on behalf of a client. I had written a similar scene in a short script in my script at film school. In the pitch meetings I had done, I'd always told the tale of the criminal and the patient lover on the outside. It had been based on a real experience of course, embellished only slightly. The story was always good for a laugh, and would someday lead to a big sale.

Now here in a small, crowded courtroom, my favorite scene was playing out, playing out for real. I forced a smile. He said he loved her. She took the plea with a smile, did the year or six months with good time and then they'd get married for real. At least there'd been a happy ending, right?

I met up with her man Troy in the gallery. He was a military man, in a tight blue t-shirt, and if he wasn't a marine, he should have been. He was about to salute, but thought better of it. He'd brought her over from overseas, but never married her. I motioned him out into the hallway.

"Sir?" he asked, in his matter-of-fact voice.

I tried to look back at Kim, who had been brought back into court. I couldn't see her petite body behind all the massive guards.

"She wants to know if you love her, if you'll wait for her if she takes the year plea."

"Sure," he said too quickly, as if he had never learned to say no during boot camp. "If that's what she needs to hear."

I looked at him again. We both caught a quick glimpse of Kim through the guards. She smiled that smile and everyone froze. For one moment, it seemed like the entire courtroom was rooting for love.

"Yeah, OK," he said after a deep breath. "I love her, I guess."

I smiled. Just like in the manuscript, except for using the word "guess."

I hurried back to Kim, this time crossing in front of the sentencing of an aggravated batterer (firearm enhancement). The judge noticed me, but kept on handing out time.

Kim rattled her leg chains nervously. "He loves you," I whispered. "He'll wait for you if you take the one year plea."

"Are you sure?"

"I guess so."

I was about to add a line from the book. "He loves you more than any man has ever loved a woman," but stopped. Instead I whispered about the risks of further angering an already angry judge.

"I need it in writing," she replied, a little too loud.

"We already have the one year plea agreement in writing."

"No, I need his word." She kept staring at me. "That he will wait for me for one year, and then we'll get married. If not I will take my chances with a full hearing."

"So if he doesn't say that he will wait one year, you're willing to risk eleven years in prison?"

"If he isn't waiting for me, if he doesn't love me, I might as well just stay inside forever," she said. "I've got to know."

I hustled back with Troy into the hallway. "She wants it in writing," I told him. "That you'll wait for her if she takes a year plea. That you'll marry her when she gets out."

"Marry her?" Suddenly, he got squeamish, as if I had asked him to sign a petition against all the wars ever fought. "I don't know if I can do that."

"What?"

"I've been with her for seven years," he said. "There's a lot you don't know. About her ... About me ..."

It would take torture to get the information out of him, or something worse to change his mind. I had to prove that I had as much control over the courtroom as I had over the computer screen. Love just had to conquer all.

I took out my pad, scribbled words of everlasting love as if I could write their script for them. "Would you just sign this for her? Please."

He thought about it, and even moved the pen ever so slightly on a bombing run toward the paper, but then aborted. "I can't, sir. I just can't."

I could sell a thousand books and free a thousand criminals, but I couldn't make love out of nothing. I looked over at Kim's eyes. Both eyes were flowing now. No matter what happened, there wouldn't be a happy ending.

The judge was so backed up that we had to do the hearing another time. The next setting, Troy was not there in the gallery. Kim ended up receiving credit for time served.

A few years later, she called me. Troy had been arrested on a drinking and driving charge.

"What are you going to do?" I asked her.

66-2-13A
AN AGGRAVATED LOVE STORY

Her name was Sky, but she was the most down-to-earth woman I had ever met. Somehow the winds had brought her from the east coast to northern New Mexico, where she worked with animals in a vet's office. I think she had a coyote in the back seat of her dusty Subaru on the day I met her. She was blonde, a youthful thirty, and her smile radiated renewable solar energy.

In my blue double-breasted suit and red tie, I didn't use words like "energy" when describing myself or others, much less the word "positive." But there we were, flirting like two high school kids in detention when the teacher wasn't looking. She mentioned *10,000 Waves,* a Japanese bathhouse in the *Sangre de Cristo* foothills. We could watch the aspens turn golden in the setting desert sun. She didn't mention anything about clothing.

Before I could answer, a guard called her name, and drew us inside. Unfortunately detention was a very real threat. We were in a magistrate court somewhere in New Mexico during a crowded docket call, and she was facing jail time, ninety days. Ninety days with sunlight might as well be an eternity to a woman like her.

"Well, counselor?" We sat before a tough looking Hispanic man, who had traded in his dark state trooper uniform for an even darker judge's robe. I thought about the aspens, but his stern tone dragged me back into the cramped courtroom. He said the word "counselor" like the English translation of the Spanish word, *pendejo*.

"As to the charge of Aggravated DWI," I said. "My client pleads NOT GUILTY."

The judge read the words "up to ninety days," and set up a "pre-trial" in a month. I thought about the potential penalties I faced if things went wrong—fired, disbarred, and broken-hearted was no way to go through life. Had I fallen in love with a client at a bond arraignment?

A few weeks later, I snuck out to Santa Fe and played hooky for the afternoon. Sky would meet me halfway. I met her at a local bookstore/coffee shop. Over cinnamon chai, she made me read her a poem by Octavio Paz called "Conduits of the sun." By the final conduit, I had already maneuvered us to the checkout, paid the thirty dollars for the entire book.

We next wandered up Canyon Road with its charming adobe galleries. I bought her blue Tibetan earrings to match her eyes. In the next gallery, she bought an abstract painting, which matched the gold in her hair. The artist pointed to the abstract female shape in the sailboat on a turbulent sea.

"Notice how the wind is blowing the sails in different directions." The artist said. "It's called *Fickle Wind Woman*."

I hugged Sky tightly, but didn't kiss her. We went back into the gathering dusk of Canyon Road, couldn't help but think briefly about the full-body frisking she'd get from the guards if I failed. The sun had already set behind the pines of the foothills, and we kept holding each other close for warmth as we walked in the crisp high altitude air. I wanted to, Lord, I wanted to, but I didn't kiss her then either. She went back to the Subaru and hugged the waiting coyote.

The next morning, my boss at the time asked me the

name of the client I had met with for four hours yesterday afternoon. He had received some documents, but didn't specify. I'm not saying he's a control freak, but in a moment of darkness, I'd joked that he'd even proofread my suicide note. I'd like to think that things were better between us, but he swiftly closed the door in his office with the other partners.

I stared at that closed white door. Had anyone seen Sky and myself together? No. Well no one that knew me or her, or that I was her lawyer. Even if they had, I hadn't kissed her, which should count for something.

Still, I'd bought her earrings, drank chai, and had read her a poem with the word "conduits" in it. Was reading the poem an appearance of impropriety?

An hour later, the door opened. The boss asked me about another case, other documents. I was happy to be in trouble for something else. I was safe for the moment, but I still had two hearings to go.

Next was her DMV hearing, where her license to drive was on the line. We talked on the phone for hours the night before and coordinated our outfits—we both wore black. My tie even matched her turquoise pin.

As we waited in the town's state office building that morning, I almost thought we were home free when the state troopers didn't show with less than a minute to go. At the last possible moment the troopers entered, reluctantly as if they were only there because of pressure from above. She smiled at them. They almost turned around and walked out when they saw that smile, but the hearing officer quickly ordered them in and commenced the hearing before they could escape.

I was a brilliant lawyer for twenty minutes.

Unfortunately, I kept on going for forty. Love could not conquer her refusal to submit to a breath test.

I was more devastated than she was. I nearly cried. As I walked out dejected, she kissed me on the cheek, her lips warm and moist. I didn't dare kiss her back. The amazed state troopers watched from across the hall.

"See you at trial, counselor," one of them said with a smirk.

Two weeks later, the day of her trial arrived. I got to court fifteen minutes early and she was nowhere to be found. I approached the ADA, a tough hometown Latina, certainly had no sympathy for a fickle wind woman, especially a blond Anglo woman named "Sky."

Perhaps we could make it go away with a plea. I tried to get the "aggravated" thrown out to get rid of the mandatory time at least.

The ADA stared at me without a shred of mercy in her brown eyes, "Why is your client different from the thirty-seven other aggravated DWIs out there?"

"She was in an accident, she wasn't thinking clearly. That's why she refused the breath test."

I talked fast. I then started talking even faster.

"I'll cut you a break," she said at last, perhaps weary of whatever it was I was saying. Some of it must have made sense. The ADA then frowned. "Is your client even here yet?"

I looked around. There was no Sky to be seen.

The ADA didn't say anything more. She didn't have to. She pointed to her watch. I hurried out and called Sky. Ring. Ring. Ring. Ring. Ring. Ring. Ring.

"Hello?" a tired voice asked. She was still in bed and she

lived over an hour and a half away. She thought it was at 11:00, and mentioned something about some "negative drama" in her life.

I had no patience for any additional drama, negative or positive. "Get over here, right away." I wanted to joke that she only had her license for another week; she certainly didn't have to worry about the consequences of speeding.

I went back to the ADA, still frowning. "She'll be here in an hour."

"She better be." the ADA replied. "I'll ask for a warrant. It's two weeks till the next docket."

The ADA went back to the docket call, and started with the seven men already in custody. I paced in the parking lot.

Still alone, I caught up with the Judge as he took a break as the first batch was sent back to the jail. He told me he couldn't talk now.

I went over to the public defender. "Talk slowly!"

But the clock kept ticking. The judge's lectures to the defendants grew shorter and shorter, but he made their sentences longer and longer.

Finally Sky arrived, out of breath, with no make-up, her blond hair messily tied in a bow. She was still the most beautiful woman I had ever seen.

"Do I have time to pee?"

I looked over at the angry ADA then shook my head.

It was touch and go before the Judge. "You've got a real sweet deal," he told her as he reviewed our paperwork. "Too sweet."

Sky squirmed in her seat, both for emotional and biological reasons. For a moment I thought he would throw it all out, but after a moment's hesitation, he signed. No jail time! Call me Moses, and let my people go!

She hugged me, right there in front of everyone. The ADA stared for a moment, but said nothing.

As we walked out into the lot, I stared at Sky, gathered up my courage. "So what are you doing next weekend?" I asked

She smiled for a moment, then checked her calendar … She was busy.

My heart sank. The sky grew cloudy; I felt a breeze come up. Was this the fickle wind that could blow her away, now that the chains were broken?

"I'm kidding," she said at last, smiling. "I had plans, but I guess they got canceled. I'm free."

"So am I."

I called the next day and left a message. Nothing. I left another message. Nothing. I was about to dial again, then I realized that there might be a fine line between true love and a temporary restraining order.

A few weeks later, I went to the airport to pick up my sister. She was there with someone—a dreadlocked guy who looked like the lead guitarist for a rap/rock band. I couldn't tell if he was arriving or departing. I knew enough not to ask if she had driven him down and risked the mandatory seven days. She came over, hugged me, said she'd been "busy," but neglected to say what she had been busy doing. Her eyes were not bloodshot, her speech was not slurred and no odor of alcohol emanated from her facial area at least. Then she and Mr. Dreadlocks disappeared into the Thanksgiving crowds.

I couldn't help but wonder—what had he defended her on?

SWEET AND SOUR ROMANCE

It ended with a great question: Should a lawyer break the law for love? It started with a simple one: How much should I tip at a Chinese Buffet?

The tipping issue came up every Wednesday at a place I'll call the Hong Kong Buffet. It was right near my gym, and I'd gorge myself after 40 minutes of free weights and Nordic Track. The place was great, unlimited portions of Pepper steak, Peking duck and a Mongolian barbeque for just $6.95 with a coupon.

Still, I was always puzzled. If you have to walk all the way up and wait in line behind five fat people for the duck on one trip, and then wait behind a family of seven for the barbeque on your next, should you tip the server an extra buck or two just for serving the beverage?

At first the answer was no … And then I met Amy.

She was a petite Chinese beauty, her long black hair pulled back tightly into a pony tail. The first thing I noticed about her was her smile. Even in her drab off-white polo shirt uniform, her smile would light up all of Mongolia.

Her English was minimal, and she carried around a pocket of Chinese-English translator machine for unfamiliar words. When I asked her how she was, she always replied "good." That one syllable somehow stretched out until I heard every rise and fall of the Great Wall itself.

As she dropped my pink lemonade, she shyly commented on how I always ate alone, always ate too quickly, and sometimes left before getting my fortune cookie.

I explained that I had to watch whatever TV show was hot at the moment, which was true for the most part. Or perhaps I didn't want to know my future.

Unfortunately those same few sentences back and forth were the extent of our conversations. She had minimal knowledge of American pop culture, much less television. In China, she hadn't even heard of *Star Wars*.

I had just broken up with a TV producer. How could I ever fall for a woman who wouldn't laugh at my Yoda imitation?

I quickly saw that she had a big heart, which more than made up for failing the Yoda test. She often had to help the worst possible patrons of a buffet—college football players. To Amy, everything was "good" and occasionally all good.

She also had a regular Wednesday table of an extended Navajo family. The Navajos had left Asia across the Arctic land bridge forty thousand years ago, yet Amy treated them as if they'd all shared tea just last weekend. Amy always had an extra treat for their youngest child, so they always greeted Amy as another member of their tribe. Unfortunately, they never left any money for her.

As I watched her hustle from table to table, I noticed that everyone loved her. To me as I munched on my ugly Peking duckling, she was the beautiful swan.

After a few Wednesdays, Amy sat down with me for a moment or two, resting her small feet between her dashes for lemonade for the linebackers and cokes for the Navajos. Over the course of the night, I learned that Amy wasn't her real name of course. She said her name in Chinese, but I failed utterly in repeating it, and certainly couldn't figure out how it could possibly have the letter "x" lurking somewhere inside it.

She was twenty-seven, but looked younger, especially when she giggled. She had grown up in a small city in China the seventh daughter of a drunken fisherman, or something like that. She had studied business but ended her schooling before coming to America, yet dreamed of owning her own business someday.

After she dropped off the fortune cookie ("Expect Surprises!"), I surprised myself by leaving a $20 bill on top of the $8.95.

The next Wednesday, she seemed very anxious. Her supervisor, a woman who must have put "sour" in sweet and sour, looked over at us. The Sour Woman shouted something at Amy in Chinese. Amy hurriedly joined the Sour Woman in the kitchen, as if it was some kind of re-education camp.

When they came out again a few minutes later, Amy looked re-educated. The Sour Woman kept staring at her as Amy, still smiling, rushed from table to table to fill all the empty glasses.

I didn't leave her a tip; I gave her my legal business card.

Thursday, my secretary buzzed me. There was someone on the phone whom she could not understand. At first she thought it was one of my juvenile clients calling collect from a foreign jail. I knew it was Amy.

I asked if she was all right. She was "good" of course, although she didn't sound it. I couldn't think of anything to say after we exchanged a few more sentences, so I surprised myself by asking her out on the next Tuesday, her only day off. She said yes immediately. I did not need her electronic translator to sense how her anxiety had lifted.

I had thought she'd slept in the kitchen, but she lived in a small house with some family members in a tough neighborhood. She waited outside and I almost didn't recognize her. Her hair was out of the pony tail, and she wore a peasant dress and a low-cut, yet sophisticated black blouse.

We went out to an upscale Mexican place and I explained the concept of blue corn enchiladas. I don't know whether this was the first time someone had ever waited on her before, but it certainly was close. When she finished her ice tea, she almost went up to get another one herself. When I told her that it would be taken care of, she had the biggest smile of her life.

I tipped the waitress well.

Fridays and Saturdays I spent dating different women, but nothing ever jelled. I went to the place on Monday, and soon I spent my Tuesday nights with Amy. She always wore the same outfit, and always had the same smile.

I never kissed Amy, but I didn't need to. That smile, that glow lit up our Tuesdays out and our Wednesdays at the restaurant. I can't remember what we talked about. We actually attempted to have a discussion about communism in China, but even with her translator machine, we never got past the word for those little "hats" that Mao made people wear.

On the Tuesday before my birthday, she surprised me with a pink teddy bear. I wondered to myself, what kind of woman would give a man a pink teddy bear. I worried that if other women came to my apartment, they would see the teddy bear and figure it was given to me by another woman, or worse, another man.

Then one Tuesday night, everything changed. We ate seafood at some New England seafood house. I think she had butterfly shrimp. I joked that she was the butterfly, and

I was the shrimp. She always pretended to laugh at my jokes, but couldn't muster the effort, just stared at the shrimp plate.

After an awkward pause, she asked me, "Are you really my friend?"

"Yes, of course."

Another long pause.

"You marry me?"

Huh? I was speechless. My own mother had said that my wedding reception was going to be held at the old age home, and I was now in a drought that had lasted over a year. Of all the women I had known, no one had ever wanted to marry me, much less me marry them.

She had a real reason of course, which took her a few awkward moments to reveal, although I guessed it immediately. She was no longer in the country legally, and faced God knows what back home.

I was hurt. My stomach was tied up in knots. Was that what this was all about? Had she thought that for a few lemonades and a pink teddy bear I would risk criminal prosecution, risk a $250,000 fine and seven years in prison, just to marry a woman I barely knew? I thought she was my friend, a real friend.

I shook my head with rage. Not good, not good at all. So much for friendship, she'd been using me all along, right? I drove her home immediately, and dropped her off by the curb.

Wednesday, Thursday, Friday, Saturday, Sunday, Monday I couldn't stop thinking of her, the smile, the giggle. There was a line in the *Simpsons* when a character had said something like, "It would be a sham marriage, but as sham marriages go it would be one of the best."

I didn't go to the restaurant on Wednesday, didn't call her the following Tuesday.

Yet, I couldn't get that smile out of my head. It wasn't the smile; it was what was behind it. I was cynical, and the worst thing in my life was not getting into Georgetown Law School. She had grown up poor in a communist dictatorship and lived in constant fear of being returned there in shackles, yet she still believed in humanity. She wasn't in the country legally; but I had dated both attorneys and exotic dancers, and neither was known for their morals. Who was I to judge?

I went back another Monday. Amy came over with her lemonade. She then told me that would have to leave in two weeks. For good. She did not say where she was going. I knew enough not to ask.

For one brief moment as I stared at those deep brown eyes, I flashed back to her playing with the little Navajo child as if it was her own, even if the family had never tipped her more than a quarter. This was a kind spirit, a woman without an evil bone in her small body.

I really thought about marrying her, and perhaps it wouldn't be a sham marriage after all. I could teach her English every day, perhaps with the help of dubbed martial arts films. I could help her financially, so she could get her education and open her business in whatever it was she wanted. I could make her see every *Star Wars* movie three times until she could tell Jabba the Hut from Jar Jar Binks.

But before I could say anything, the Navajos wanted to try their hands at chopsticks and she vanished again.

The Sour Woman watched her as five more groups vied for four tables in her section. I left her a twenty and didn't wait for my fortune cookie.

I was there for her last Monday in America. It must have been the most crowded Monday in the buffet's history. Yet, she stopped at all her regular tables to have a picture taken with them.

She smiled and took me to the party room. She reluctantly got the Sour Woman to take our picture against a photographic backdrop of the gleaming Hong Kong Skyline. In that moment I felt we were on top of the hundred stories of the famed Bank of China Tower, staring down at the fragrant harbor below. The light flashed, and then it took me a moment for my eyes to adjust.

Before my eyes could focus, the Sour Woman then said something to Amy in Chinese. When my eyes opened, she was gone.

She called me the next night at ten o'clock. She didn't say where she was. The picture was ready. She called me right during the middle of my favorite TV show. I couldn't leave. I told her I'd pick it up at the restaurant the next day. She said she didn't know if she could be there, but she'd try.

That Thursday, I went back to the restaurant. It was only 6, but I was too late. Amy was gone to parts unknown.

The Sour Woman showed me two pictures, one of us and one of her in her black outfit.

I was surprised by my own emotion. I wiped the tear in my eye away before the Sour Woman could see it. No it wouldn't have been a sham after all. That night I ate in silence. My waiter didn't smile and never brought me a refill of my lemonade.

As I got up to leave, before the fortune cookie of course, I stopped to wonder again just how much you are supposed to tip at a buffet.

By the time I was thirty-four, after a few close calls, I put the book on the back-burner and totally concentrated on the law. I finally moved out of my dad's basement into a real office downtown, right next to Metropolitan court. I still didn't have a secretary, but my phone was ringing from my forty dollar a month ad in the yellow pages under "juvenile lawyers."

My only contact with show business was that I'd go off to the movies every Friday and I feared my only communication would be to ask for butter with my popcorn.

Ironically, as I finally started making a name for myself, I started to realize the costs of becoming a successful lawyer.

LAW AND POWDER

I would argue a case before the esteemed New Mexico Supreme Court in Santa Fe in the morning and then ski through the trees at the picturesque Ski Santa Fe resort in the afternoon. That was my dream, and it was about to come true. The legendary Deon Sanders had played baseball and football in the same year, but as far as I knew, no one had ever helped shape the law of the land while wearing skier's thermal underwear under his double-breasted suit.

This wasn't a mere act of bravado or a desperate attempt at retaining my fading youth, this had context. At the University of Colorado, I had once learned the rules of evidence on flashcards while going up the chairlift at Arapahoe Basin after a record spring snowfall. Unfortunately, the card for Rule 801, and at least two of the hearsay exceptions had slipped out of my mittened hand into a deep canyon halfway up the lift.

The day of the hearing, I drove the sixty miles up I-25 to the courthouse with my skis already on the rack. When I arrived at the courthouse, I felt a little skittish in light of a recent string of burglaries in Santa Fe. I decided to lock the skis in the back of my car. The Security Guard stared at the odd spectacle of a guy in a suit, sweating profusely as he tried to jab 190 centimeters of K2 into 189 centimeters of Saturn SL coupe.

Luckily, the hearing was early in the morning, because I'd still be able to make the half-hour drive to be just in time for the 12:30 half-day. I paced anxiously outside the courthouse as the court first had to hold arguments in another case, death penalty appeal or something. My case was about urine samples.

I wanted to tell them to hurry. Life, death, and freedom, whatever … just get it over with. There were eight inches of fresh powder in the tree runs off the triple chair. Those eight inches were calling my name.

I stopped thinking about the virgin white snow as I reviewed my crumpled yellow notes for the hundredth time, then silently mouthed the words for the hundred and first. I had actually practiced my answers to questions while skiing at Taos Ski Valley the weekend before, and had nearly run into an aspen tree on Al's Run.

I sweated slightly in my long-johns, but somehow the thrill of the upcoming powder kept me cool. A short time later we went into court and the hearing began in earnest. The Attorney General went first with the State's case. He looked tight, even though he probably argued here every day. He didn't seem to get any flow as he talked about case after case after case in precedent.

When it was finally my turn to speak, I felt relatively relaxed. Like going down the "green circle" of a beginner run, I anticipated the questions, much as I had anticipated the moguls from a mile away. I spoke from the heart as I talked about it being time for the law to "take a new turn."

The justices smiled. It was all downhill after that, so to speak. After the gavel came down, the justices shuffled out a back door. No decision would be reached that day, so I hurried out the door. I was going to change in the car, but I thought better of it as I eyed the security guard. I brought my crumpled ski pants into the court's washroom. In one of the other stalls, someone, perhaps a Justice, changed out of his robes into pantyhose.

I kept the skis in the car, and they kept clanging into my suit hanger as I drove the windy road up to the mountain. When I arrived at the ski area base, it was thirty degrees cooler and that was before wind chill, which in this case was also "blizzard chill." I hadn't dressed warmly enough and lasted only three runs off of the summit before calling it a day ...

In the lodge, I gulped three cups of hot chocolate to shake the chill off and bring some warmth to my extremities, all my extremities. It was that cold. As I drove back, I sniffled, sensing the avalanche of an incoming flu.

Come to think of it, I had only received a 75 in Evidence. The flashcards hadn't helped that much after my fingers got frost-nipped.

A year later, the decision came down from the court. I had won the case. I'd like to think that my effort to stay relaxed contributed to my oral argument.

I haven't been back to the New Mexico Supreme Court since that day. Every time I go skiing in Santa Fe, I can't help but think of my contribution to the law. The case made the law books. Lawyers cite the case in their briefs and arguments. I'm sure that a man is now out of prison because of the decision.

I hope he goes skiing once he gets out.

WHO ISN'T WHO?

"I would not join a club that would have me as a member."
Groucho Marx.

I myself have been selected for various *Who's Who* type publications. My biography is available for viewing in a hard-bound edition available for sale for two or three hundred dollars. Or so they tell me. I can't afford my own copy.

I don't know how I was selected for any of those publications. I have made but one contribution to the common law, <u>State v. Hodge et al</u>, 882 P.2d 1, 118 N.M. 410, which deals with preserving issues on appeal for urine samples. I don't make this stuff up.

One day, on the phone with the mother of an aggravated batterer discussing a Thanksgiving furlough, my call-waiting kicked in. I switched lines; a woman congratulated me for making the list of an honorary professional directory. I wasn't sure what she meant, I kept waiting for her to ask me about saving money on my long distance. I grew impatient. My other line clicked ominously, the mother of the aggravated batterer was not one to be kept waiting. But I was intrigued and listened to the pitch.

Apparently, a previous inductee referred me. When I asked who this person was, she told me that such information was confidential. (They told me I had to be on a "need to know basis") After going through the rest of her canned speech, she told me she'd send me the application if I was interested.

Call it vanity, but I agreed.

When I called back the mother of the aggravated burglar and told her my good fortune, she wondered if my new professional clout would help her son's case.

I filled out the application listing my biography, including of course my accomplishments in the laws of bodily fluids. I pondered whether I should include the disastrous summer job that I had in Chicago six years before, but left it blank.

I sent in my entry. A few weeks later, I received a nice letter allowing me to order the book for several hundred dollars, and a "special deluxe edition" for several hundred more. I declined.

I did get a nice plaque, which I have nowhere to put. The plaque now sits under that highly marketable screenplay I wrote about the Carthaginian army during the Second Punic war in 219 B.C.

Once I got into one publication, others quickly followed. I am honestly not sure which ones I'm in. I did check out a recent *Marquis Who's Who*, which was *not* the one that selected me. At random, I turned to pages 646-47. The longest entry on the page belongs to Charles William Cline, a poet and literary educator. He had forty lines listing accomplishments and publications. A lawyer named Gordon Clinton, originally from Medicine Hat, Alberta, had a very respectable thirty-one lines. He was sandwiched between two apparently lesser lawyers—a woman named Hillary Clinton who had twenty-five lines of text, and someone named William Jefferson Clinton, who had a mere fifteen.

I have fewer lines than that of course, but if I included the disastrous summer job in Chicago, and this story you're reading now, I might have a longer listing than both of the

Clintons combined.

In terms of business, the listing has yet to bring in a single phone call. It's listed on the resume, but no interviewer has ever commented on it. I did mention my status during a happy hour to an attractive young lawyer, but she seemed more impressed with the stockbroker who wasn't a who, but did own a Porsche.

Perhaps my lack of fame is because of a lack of getting the word out. Since I don't advertise, I haven't attempted to market myself, although I do have a catchy jingle.

"Hire me and you can't lose!
I'm in three separate editions of <u>Who's Who</u>."

So for these types of publications, find out the how, what and the why, before you're convinced there's really a who.

(Barrister)

MY FOURTEEN MINUTES

"That's who I want to be," I said to my neighbor. We were at her apartment watching actor Richard Gere in the film *Primal Fear*. She was a big Richard Gere fan, and the film had been the only thing we could agree on that night. Gere played a big-time lawyer defending a young client on murder charges.

At thirty-four, I often felt that I was play-acting rather than layering and my script was repetitive. Over and over I told the Judge that "my client has outstanding potential" as I prayed that Mr. Outstanding Potential's check didn't bounce. My biggest case at the moment was a seventeen year old kid on the heinous charge of "not paying fines." That client offered such lame excuses; he couldn't even get a Golden Globe for best liar in a misdemeanor.

My date stroked my shoulder, but I worried that she was thinking of Gere rather than me with each stroke. As she stared lovingly on that handsome smile on the screen, I pressed the pause button. I shut my eyes and made a wish.

"Someday," I said out loud. "That's gonna be me."

Be careful what you wish for.

The next day I got a call from a potential client, on the "motion to reconsider" of a very high profile case. I'd liked the guy the last time, so I offered to do the case without charge. Motions to reconsider generally fail so I figured we'd have one hearing; I'd try my heart out; and my defeat would be mentioned on page D1 of the local paper.

Life litigated art. Like any movie lawyer, as I read the man's psychological files, I started to believe in him. He had indeed changed his life from the days of his supposed crime. I even convinced myself that he might have been truly innocent of the crime in the first place. If only I'd been his lawyer back then. It was time to make things right!

Now that I had a potentially innocent client, I had a writer's block. How do I tell the world that someone had changed his life? There had to be a magic word, somewhere. It was time to write a new script.

After a few more blocked nights, my eureka moment came on the "Nordic Trek" at my health club. Ironically, I remembered an old screenplay of mine with a long speech about redemption on page ninety-seven. Redemption was always a magic word to me.

I didn't even finish my workout, headed home and found the tattered script in a moldy trunk. Still sweaty, I stuck the paragraph nearly verbatim into my handwritten draft of my opening and closing arguments. I hoped the words would sound better than they read. The old script had already been rejected by two agents, and had faltered in the preliminary rounds of an amateur screenplay competition.

As I walked into the courthouse the next morning, I got into character. I was ready for my close-up, Mr. Demille.

I had asked my client the title of his favorite song. Soon a nasty rap song played during my every waking moment. I took myself to an angry place in my heart with every rhyme. My client had been denied counseling growing up. Well, a big film conglomerate had not renewed my option. We had a lot in common. The conglomerate's coverage notes said I wasn't "compelling or commercial." Well, damn it; neither was my client!

Until now …

I recited my opening again and again under my breath as

I noticed that two of the three stations had their news vans. The reporters were setting up as I went through the door, so thankfully they did not get me on tape. I could feel the weight of their cameras as they shot through the glass window on the door.

The hearing went well, real well, even if the close-up was on the back of my neck. After my redemption speech, the judge nodded in agreement. Unfortunately, the case wasn't over yet. The judge wanted some more lawyering on both sides before he'd reach a decision. The issues were extremely technical. I would actually have to do some intensive research. I groaned; I didn't have any old scripts in my trunk on the subject of legislative intent on a law passed twenty years ago.

I was surprised when I woke up that morning. This was a bigger deal than I had ever imagined. My words were plastered over page A1 of the leading newspaper in the state, and made it all along the wire all way to *USA Today* someone told me. But they didn't mention my name, the bastards.

Later, I went to the Law Library to start reading. Other lawyers in the library pointed at me. "That's the guy with the big murder case." When I called my machine, I had calls from all three local TV stations. I hurried home because I didn't want to do interviews in the library basement payphone with some college kid waiting in line to call his girlfriend.

When I got back to the office, there were still more calls, and more calls came as I retrieved the existing ones. I must have lost one potential client for every time I said, "It's channel 7, I've got to go."

Frazzled, but in a good way, I had another date that

night with the Richard Gere fan. Trust me it is good news when you see your name on TV during a dinner date. It is even better to have someone read a story in the newspaper to you at breakfast the next morning.

Later, that afternoon, I went back to see my client in the holding area before court. The other criminals stared at me. I'd forgotten they had TV in jail. The boys in orange jumpsuits nodded at my client, lucky you. Behind me, one of the guards, or was it one of the criminals, asked how it felt to be famous.

"I wouldn't know," I muttered with false modesty. But I did know. It felt great.

I spoke too soon. The second hearing, call it the sequel, did not go so well. The State brought up some more technical issues and something about "legislative intent." The victim's family stared at the judge with daggers. I may have believed that my client was innocent, but they sure didn't.

The ADA droned on for twenty dry minutes, all substance no style. But their substance hit the target audience. The judge deferred judgment after still more research was done. That afternoon, I called some appellate experts and stayed on the line for over an hour. We were making law—in our tortured interpretations of old appellate decisions the case would be won or lost.

I talked with my mouth full of Doritos as I spoke with the experts about collateral estoppel. This was the scene that would be cut out of any re-enactment. My call-waiting buzzed several times, I missed two potential clients and now had been collaterally estopped by my soon-to-be ex-girlfriend.

I didn't worry too much. There was a call from a female

voice. "I've seen you at the gym a few times." she said with a slight giggle. "I didn't know you were so famous."

The final chapter took place a week later. Thanks to the help of the appellate lawyers, I was well prepared. I wasn't flashy, my U.S. Supreme Court decisions were just better than their State Supreme Court ones on the issue of legislative intent. The Judge did not hesitate in ruling this time. Once some paperwork was drawn up and signed, my client would be released. Free at last, free at last, great God almighty and against all odds, my client was free at last!

My client was escorted back to the holding cell. He passed right in front of me. The camera shot me from behind as I shook his hand.

A pack of reporters suddenly ambushed me. "How do you feel?" asked one. "How do you feel?" asked another. I felt like I was at the Academy Awards on the red carpet in a choppy sea of big cameras and bright lights. I took a deep breath, about to bask in the glow of my triumph. Before I could say anything, I caught a glimpse of the victim's family as they walked off with the Prosecutor, their heads hung low, totally crushed. This was no time to gloat. I might have believed in my client, but they sure didn't.

The camera was still rolling. I muttered something vague about "being happy for my client," and something even vaguer about "redemption," then walked off after a few more "no comments." When I had used the word redemption, I don't know whether I was referring to my client or myself.

I made all three stations that night. A few days later, my client was released to Alabama. They didn't have the clip of him so they showed the clip of me shaking his hand. The victim's cousin said about something about how it was a "sad day for justice."

I didn't catch it all, I was so famous that I was already bored with being famous.

The next week, I became famous somewhere else. My client moved to the Alabama and the local stations there started interviewing me at their outlets in my town. A producer with a mellifluous southern accent asked me if I wished to appear on camera. I immediately agreed.

The producer, his voice still sounding like a hypnotist, told me to stand by for a minute and a half. A minute and a half later I was in hell. All my "getting into character" was lost as my close-up became an anal probe. The host criticized me, my client, and within minutes I was unceremoniously booted off the air. I had just got my ass kicked in Alabama.

It didn't get to me, because even though several hundred thousand people heard me, no one knew me. If you get your ass kicked in Alabama and no one knows who you are, do you still make a sound?

As I went to the gym the next day, I saw the woman who had called me. She was on the stationary bike pedaling away; her eyes were transfixed on the local news.

Another horrible crime and a suspect had been arrested. An attorney we knew uttered a terse comment about his client's innocence.

She stared at the screen. "Did you hear about this case?" she said between deep breaths caused by pedaling at level 11. "I know that lawyer."

I got on the Nordic Trek next to her. I was going to ride fifteen minutes, but I was tired. I stopped at fourteen.

CAT SCRATCH LAWYER

"Your landlord repossessed your cat?" I asked Josie.

"Well, they like totally took Mr. Snuggles," Josie said. Josie was twenty-one, but came across as more of a slightly underweight kitten, with reddish brown hair, and soft green eyes. She was like a stray; she could hug you in an instant, and then claw your eyes out.

At this age, I was just happy to actually be out at a real life party after nine o'clock. Especially an Albuquerque party filled with models, photographers, graphic designers and what not. I think the hostess had given me an invitation by mistake after I represented her cousin on a DWI. Still, I could pretend I was at a sophisticated soiree in LA, but with better parking. The fact that I was now talking to a beautiful woman dressed in a black cocktail dress made it even better.

Josie practically purred at me as she related attempts at paying her rent on time, to no avail. The evil landlord, a Scandinavian Snidely Whiplash, had already taken her cute little cat and dumped it at some mysterious building down town. She didn't know whether it was still alive or worse, being used in fiendish experiments at the local Veterinary Assistant School. Her soft green eyes clouded up with tears right on cue.

I did what every red blooded lawyer would do. "I'll write a letter to your landlord to get your cat back," I said.

She smiled with perfect white teeth, a Cheshire grin. "Thank you! Thank you!"

"I'll help you in any way I can," I said, way too quickly.

"Any way?"

"I guess so." I looked into her green eyes and I knew I was already lost. I gave her my card with the words "Attorney at law following my name."

"It's all good."

I had never been "all good" before, especially this late at night, with someone this young. "I won't charge you any legal fees either," I said. "Call me."

Before she could respond, she saw something out of the corner of her eye, as if spying a mouse. She suddenly bounded over to the other side of the room. He was dressed in leather and had the aura of a mad dog. She sat on his lap as if she belonged there. He petted her hair, possessively. He glared at me. I had overstayed my welcome in impolite society and it was only nine: fifteen.

I left, thinking I'd never hear from her ever again. She was someone else's pet of the month, or at least of the night.

I was surprised when my phone rang that Tuesday afternoon. I was stuck on the interstate after a two-thirty meeting with the parents of a man accused of aggravated fleeing. I hadn't known that fleeing could be aggravated. I sweated in my dark suit; New Mexico had never been this humid. I wanted to do an aggravated flee of Albuquerque for cooler temperatures.

The phone rang again.

"Yeah?" I shouted into the phone.

"It's Josie," a soft voice whispered. "From the party."

Where had I heard the name Josie before? I thought about a cartoon, *Josie and the Pussy Cats*. I hadn't remembered if the cartoon Josie was a woman or a real cat.

"Josie?"

She then did that famous purr and my memories rushed

back. "Why don't you come over to see me? I'm on the west side."

I took the next exit and switched directions on the freeway. This dog day afternoon could still be salvaged.

As I crossed over the Rio Grande, I smiled a Cheshire grin of my own. She hadn't mentioned a letter at all, perhaps she had been overwhelmed by my charm, or perhaps she was just—what do they call it when cats get excited?

In heat, right?

I arrived at her gigantic apartment complex on the west side of town off the Coors Bypass. I had always wondered why a city with a drunken driving problem had named a major thoroughfare after an alcohol magnate family.

She just said she would meet me, "by the office." I finally found a building with an American flag at half-mast. This must be it. I wondered who had died.

I got out of my car, took my suit jacket off, but kept my tie on. With the humidity, I felt like a missionary in some place like Bangkok. Some tough gang kids stared. They certainly wouldn't be converted by the likes of me.

Suddenly Josie appeared, as if she had jumped down from the pine tree behind me. Had she been watching me all along?

She was stunning in her pink tank top; her petite, toned body was tan in the setting sun. She had a slight glow to her from the humidity. That made her even sexier. Her eyes were a paler shade of green with just a hint of blood in the corners, as if she'd been crying.

A tough-looking kid rode by us in his bicycle. He snickered. What was he thinking? She was my mistress? She was my daughter? She was my whore?

She gave me a hug; I felt the moisture of her arms through my shirt. It was a hard hug to read. She whispered something in my ear in her soft voice.

Maybe I was getting old. "What?" I asked. She whispered again, and then laughed, that infectious laugh.

"Will you buy a cat for me?"

My car felt like a litter box with the papers, and work-out clothes. I had to clear away the day's paperwork in the front of my car. I tossed a Judgment and Sentence for a probation violation, and then an Entry of Appearance for the Fleeing into the back seat. I wiped away a few chewed off pens before I finally felt it was clean enough for her perfect rear end. As we turned onto Coors Bypass, I went out of my way to tell her that just because I was buying her a cat, didn't mean that I had any expectation of anything else from her.

I told her that again and again. I wanted to avoid even the appearance of impropriety. I was too embarrassed to even bring up *Josie and the Pussy Cats.*

She smiled again before I said anything. "It's all good."

I wasn't quite sure what she meant by that. What was all? What was good?

We crossed the bypass to the gigantic pet store across the street. It had enough supplies inside for a small zoo. Despite the store's size, Josie knew the exact location of the cats.

I gasped at a sign on the wall. Cats may have been born free, but to release them would cost me nearly a hundred dollars up front. I shuddered. I had taken drunken driving cases for less than the cost of a cat.

Before I could say anything, about buying a goldfish instead; she had opened the cage and held a cat in her hand. She stroked its fur.

For one moment, she looked peaceful.

Something was wrong. The cat didn't really respond to her. She was a bit too rough, the cat sensed it.

The cat spit something up. It would rather stay in a cage than leave with her.

After she petted it a few more times, she sensed that there was no connection either. "I don't want this one," she said. "Let's go."

I smiled. I had just saved ninety-five dollars. Perhaps we could now switch our attention to other matters. The cat might not have liked her, but I still did. Appearance of impropriety be damned.

"Maybe we can do this another time," I said. "I'll take you to a nice dinner."

"Not yet," she said. "I know of another place. More cats. On the other side of town."

Traversing to the other side of town in rush hour sounded like crossing the savannah on a safari. I'd need a National Geographic explorer grant to pay for the team. I started to whimper.

She then gave me a look with those big green eyes, and another purr.

We found a smaller, more intimate pet store on the other side of town. I had barely made it inside before she spotted the perfect kitten. The kitten must have walked through the walls, because it was in Josie's hand instantly as if rushing for his mother. No, that wasn't it, Josie and the kitten connected on a deeper level. They had been long, lost litter mates.

I could not deny the love in her eyes. For the first time, she looked truly happy. Everything indeed was all good.

I felt warm inside. I was doing a good thing for someone in trouble.

"Twenty bucks," the owner said.

My wallet was already out. I didn't even have to pay tax either.

The store owner put the kitten in the box. Josie petted it a few more times, but the kitten suddenly grew agitated.

When we got back in the car, the agitation grew worse. My allergies suddenly kicked in. Who knew where this kitten had been? Or what it had eaten? The cat clawed at my crotch nearly penetrating the nice fabric of my suit pants. I feared that the kitten's young claws would scratch something else for a moment. I was about to shoo it away, but I felt self-conscious.

She laughed a cute laugh. "Here kitty," she said. "Here kitty."

The kitten jumped over to her, for just a moment, as if sensing instinctively that it had a new and loving mom. I had to slam the breaks at the light on 19th street. The kitten fell to the floor. It then bounded to the back seat and began clawing at my legal documents. I was scared the kitten would crap on my appeal before the Court of Appeals had its turn.

The kitten was clearly out of control.

Why is rush hour always the worst on hot, humid days? The allergies made the air even thicker, and not just for me. The kitten jumped into a window, thinking it was a way out. I finally did some fancy driving and made it back to her apartment. The flag in front of the office was now gone for the day.

"We won't be that long," Josie said. Was she mad at me?

She vanished before I could figure out which apartment

she lived in. Meanwhile, I quickly changed out of my suit into shorts and a black Bruce Springsteen t-shirt.

I suddenly shivered at the age difference between us.

"Glory days. They pass you by. Glory Days. In the wink of a young girl's eye." Bruce sang in my head. He had first sung those words before Josie had been born.

I started to worry when she didn't come down immediately. She came down a few minutes later. Were there scratches on her arm? For a second, I wondered if they were track marks. I didn't really know this woman that well, after all.

Before I could ask, she smiled at me again. "Let's eat," she said seductively. "I could eat a horse."

I wondered whether horse meat was legal in New Mexico. Cock fighting still was, so maybe. She touched my hand again. I was definitely hooked now. Horse, let's see, I think there was an ethnic market on the east side that sold just about anything. I looked out on the traffic on the bypass. The east side was out of the question at this hour.

"Is there anything nearby?"

"There's a seafood place by the mall," she said. "I love sea food."

Her eyes lit up. I couldn't help but think of a cat eying my dad's aquarium. At the restaurant, we ordered ten oysters as an appetizer. Ordering oysters certainly gave the appearance of impropriety, but she didn't care for my canons. She ate like she didn't eat on a regular basis and didn't know where her next meal was coming from. She was hungry, real hungry.

We talked between slurps. By her third oyster, she revealed a lot of her issues. She was a bit of a stray cat, herself, adopted by a bad family, and then shuffled off to another. I didn't know if she'd received all her shots either.

"No one ever held me growing up," she said over her fourth oyster, her eyes clouding for just an instant. Her eyes hinted that I might be the one to hold her. She revealed that she did have a boyfriend, but it was "so over."

I thought a bit about the guy she'd been with at the party —the guy with the mad dog eyes. Was he the boyfriend? He didn't hold her like it was so over.

I couldn't read her. It wasn't just the oysters that affected me. She was a beautiful young lady. Still, I felt like we were playing a game of cat and mouse, and I was feeling more like Mickey.

She purred again. "We gotta go to Walmart to buy cat stuff."

I frowned, but she touched my hand again. "Please. You're a lawyer, you can afford it."

I knew I didn't have a good rebuttal argument to that one. Oh well, I knew I couldn't let the kitten starve, now could I?

As we wandered through the massive aisles of a Walmart super center, I felt like a rat even more so, a rat in some strange experiment. Josie hinted that she needed some clothes in aisle seven. Before I could say anything, she threw some sexy underwear into the cart.

"It's only nine bucks." She said.

The yellow smiley face Walmart mascot laughed in my face. She threw in a bra, and then another. "It's on sale," she said as if that made everything all right. "Two for one."

I then remembered that I had once represented a man who bought lunch for a woman at McDonalds and she exchanged a sexual favor for a Big Mac with extra cheese.

The cops knew she was a prostitute and asked her if the only reason she had slept with him was the food.

Without hesitation she had said yes. He had a conviction and six months' probation. I wondered what my former client would have received if he had supersized the combo.

I wasn't violating the canons of ethics, but I didn't know about the New Mexico Revised Statutes, Annotated. I suddenly shuddered.

I made it a point to tell her "Just because I'm buying you this stuff, doesn't mean I expect anything from you. I'm just doing this as a good Samaritan."

A Good Samaritan didn't buy a cat for hot chick, much less cat food. The elderly greeter stared at us and shook her head.

Josie didn't say anything. She moved the cart down to Aisle Eight.

One-hundred dollars later, I passed through the Walmart exit. The greeter checked every purchase I made and matched it to the receipt. I half expected her to ask me if I had a receipt for the girl.

Any lingering effect of the oysters was long gone. I just wanted the evening to be over. We got to my car as the sun was almost down in the west. I opened the door for Josie. She nodded at me. She appreciated that I was a gentleman.

I relaxed for one moment. This was just one of those funny experiences to tell to your buddies in a worst date ever session.

But then the worst date ever got even worse.

Josie's phone blasted some angry rap song. It most definitely wasn't Bruce Springsteen. Before I could even leave the parking space, she yelled at the person on the other side and then hung up abruptly.

She suddenly started wailing.

"Take me to a pay phone!" She demanded. "My phone doesn't make outgoing calls."

She jumped out of the car. She dodged Walmart traffic and made it over to the one working payphone in the entire complex.

She swore, and then slammed the phone hard, very hard. I suddenly grew very afraid. She got back in the car. I started the motor and eased into traffic. She took another call, started yelling again. She now was making a weird shrieking noise, a cat on a hot tin roof, or in this case a hot tin Saturn coupe. I tried to cover my ears until I remembered that I was driving.

"Take me to another pay phone!"

She didn't say please. I couldn't help but look down at her sharp nails. She could most definitely draw blood. I was now very, very afraid. "Let me just take you home."

She shrieked for her reply.

My mind raced through the DSM 1, 2, 3, 4 and 5 in an attempt to diagnose her. I remembered where I had seen this behavior. She was mimicking what her kitten had done in my car. She now swung her fists wildly. She hit my mirror, but thankfully didn't break it.

"Please calm down," I said, too nervous to be much of a shrink.

She didn't calm down. She swung again, I ducked. I swerved out of my lane. I nearly hit a Jaguar. It would have been a catastrophe. I nearly went catatonic with fear. Was this what Ted Nugent was talking about in *Cat Scratch Fever?*

I finally navigated the way back to her apartment. Her shrieking got worse. I wondered what people were thinking, that I was kidnapping her, or worse?

We pulled to a stop and she jumped out of the car. I had no idea what she was saying out loud. She probably had no idea what she was saying. The DSM-IV would call it transference. She had apparently confused me with her evil boyfriend. She had forgotten that I had bought her the cat. I was now her enemy, her prey, her mouse.

I meekly asked her if she wanted me to take the litter box up.

"No. Stay away from me!"

She then head butted my car, right above the passenger window. I think she dented it. The gang kid on the bicycle pedaled over from his part of the parking lot. He looked like he had seen this before.

"Are you all right?" I asked. "Do you want me to call 911?"

I remembered one rule of 911—somebody always gets arrested. This had stopped being funny.

"No!" she screamed. She head butted my car again like she was a lion attacking the vehicle on an ill-fated safari.

I picked up the litter box from my car and placed it on the ground. I then got back into my car, slammed the door and hurried off into the sunset. Only moments later, fifty feet down the bypass, my phone rang again.

"Josie?" I asked. "Are you all right?"

Luckily, it was a client. "What's going on with my case?"

I didn't hear the name; it was either the trafficker of meth facing nine years or the traffic ticket warrant facing ninety dollars.

"I don't really know right now," I said. "I'm not at my office."

I looked back at the complex. For a second I thought she was chasing after me, but it was a female jogger. Traffic was so bad that the jogger actually passed me.

An hour later, I made it home, alive. Without air conditioning that night, I was the cat in a hot brick loft. I had all kinds of panic attacks and could not sleep. Would she kill herself? Would her boyfriend kill her? Would she kill her cat?

I then had an even worse fear. She could say anything she wanted that night. Other than the gang kid on the bike, there were no witnesses to anything. Suppose she did get a bump on the head and blamed me? My career would be ruined. Appearance of impropriety was a vengeful bitch.

I didn't sleep at all waiting for the cops to come and take me away.

The next morning I was in court by eight thirty for a shooting at or from a motor vehicle. Something was wrong. There were cops everywhere. There were cameras everywhere. There were even cops with cameras.

I hurried over to the information desk. The clerk told me that the attention was for the sentencing of a mentally ill killer. "Thank God!" I said when I found out that the mentally ill killer was a man and not a woman.

While at the desk, I couldn't help but look up Josie. Sure enough she had a warrant. Failure to appear. When did I start hanging out with women with warrants?

The clerk stared at me. "Is something wrong?"

"I don't know," I said.

I made it through the rest of the day without incident. I didn't sleep that night either, not even a cat nap.

There were cameras in court the next day, I cringed until I found out it was for an embezzling case. I still felt that the cameras could penetrate to the uneasiness of my soul.

I finally received a call the next day over lunch at a cheap Japanese restaurant. I was very much alone of course and didn't worry about spilling my sashimi on my lap.

I finally picked up the phone, which seemed to be hiding under a tuna roll. Private number. I took a risk and answered.

"It's Josie," she said.

This woman sounded too normal. I almost didn't recognize her. "Uh, Josie the cat girl?" I asked.

"Yeah, sorry about that night," she said, "When my old boyfriend calls, it like freaks me out, but it's all good. I'm switching medications too."

She went on about how her old boyfriend affected her and her dosages. Ironically, seeing the cat back at her apartment had calmed her down. Assuming that the boyfriend would have called anyway, perhaps I really had saved her life. I wasn't totally sure if that was a good thing.

"Well, good luck," I said. I wanted the conversation to end.

"One more thing," she said at last.

"Yeah?"

"So what are you doing tonight?"

I was about to hang up, but then she did that purr again.

SCARED STRAIGHT

"Where do I know you from," I asked the Christina Aguilera-look alike. We were in the hallway of a children's court in New Mexico. She stood alone, dressed conservatively in black and white, holding a beautiful toddler. Early twenties, she looked a little old to be here among the juvenile delinquents. Was she a law student? Was she someone's secretary? Had I tried to pick up on her in a bar using my lame "I'm a lawyer but I'm also a writer" routine?

She cast her eyes downward. Her baby copied her expression. "I don't think so," she said, eyes still down. She was not happy to see me, whoever she was. "You must be confusing me with someone else."

Before I could inquire further, she quickly spun to the left and danced through the crowd and entered the cramped courtroom. I decided that she was probably a social work graduate student that I knew through a friend, probably here on her internship and stuck without a sitter. I knew this would haunt me for the rest of the docket. I sniffled over a lingering, strangely familiar scent for a moment.

"So are you back from Hollywood for good?" A lawyer in a brown polyester suit interrupted my reverie. "Did you miss us?"

"Sure, I missed all of this," I said in a voice that barely masked the sarcasm. I was about to launch into my exciting adventures over the last two years, but glanced at my watch. "Got a paying client, the whole *scared straight* thing."

I turned without another word and hurried to meet my

party. My paying client was a young man with relatively minor "incident reports" He wouldn't even go before the judge, just a probation officer on the other side of the building. I had promised his mother that I would give him my own personal "scared straight" tour—show him around the Juvenile Justice Center, point out a few real live scary criminals to open his eyes. Just like exposing Malcolm McDowell to an overdose of the ultra-violence in *Clockwork Orange* was supposed to rid him of his anti-social tendencies.

They were already waiting when I entered the courthouse. He wore a white polo shirt, looking much younger than his sixteen years. His mother was in her Sunday best, mortified that her friends from church might find out about this. His meeting with the probation officer was uneventful. Sure enough, his charges would not be forwarded onto the children's court attorney. I didn't have to say anything after "Sorry I'm late."

The boy was relieved that this was over, but his mother was disappointed. This was hardly the fire and brimstone she felt her son needed. She looked over at me and nodded. "You said you'd show him around."

I smiled at them both. "So son, are you ready to get *scared straight?*"

He nodded, excited in spite of it all. This would be like sneaking into an R-rated movie with his mom's permission. I would be an usher in a four hundred dollar Glen Plaid suit.

We went to the crowded courtroom and found a seat in the front row of the gallery. He was the only one wearing a shirt with a collar, his mother was the only one wearing a dress below the knees without tattoos. My client recognized one of the kids from his gym class and was about to wave, before his mother grabbed his arm. "Don't associate with those people," she said. Thankfully, no one heard.

Christina sat by the aisle and didn't look up as we slid past her onto the wooden benches of the gallery. As I brushed past her, her perfume jogged my memory. I knew her all right, even "associated" with her. She wasn't a social work graduate student, not as far as I knew, she was a woman I'd met at a St. Patrick's Day party in my apartment complex, in that three bedroom unit that was right next to the freeway. I didn't know her last name, much less what she did, but she wore high heels and a short skirt and followed me the hundred yards home for a one night stand from a few weeks back. She really was just a *one night stand;* we had never actually gotten horizontal.

"I don't meet many guys like you," she said. "Nice guys with real jobs."

She had come back to my place, kissed me and then took a call before vanishing abruptly into the night. She mumbled something about someone picking her up in the parking lot.

I didn't know what to think. Was my breath really that bad?

"I just have to see someone right now," she'd said, as she ran down the stairs. "It's not you, it's me."

As I took a good long look at her now, in the bright glare of the courtroom lights, I couldn't help but smile as I pictured the little dragon tattoo on the back of her neck.

If God was punishing me for smiling, the door opened, and the perfume smothered my face again with the draft. Like a Pavlov dog, I coughed, sharp bursts. My client and his mother looked over at me. Under his mother's glare, I suddenly felt like I was the one who was naked.

"You look like you've seen a ghost," the mother whispered.

"It's nothing. I'm fine." I protested a bit too much.

Up at the podium, a sixteen year old was slapped on the wrist for bowling after curfew. His sentence—more community service and no bowling. So much for the ultra-violence.

My client looked at me with a scowl. "Is this it?" he said with his eyes. He wanted to see something bloodier. So did his mom.

And for that matter, so did I.

Christina looked down at a copy of the day's docket, searching for a name. That's when the judge called the next case. A silence gripped the room. Two beefy armed guards dragged in a prisoner from the holding area, his shackles clanked with every forced step. The prisoner looked about twenty-one; his head was shaved, tattoos everywhere including a small one on the back of his neck that I couldn't make out. He wore a dark blue jumpsuit from the downtown Adult facility. Every probation officer and every attorney tensed. This was King Kong in the courtroom, right before the great ape smashed through his shackles and made a break for it.

My client looked around at all the commotion. He smiled at me with nervous anticipation. This is what he wanted to see. His mother put a protective hand on his shoulder.

That's when I noticed that Christina and the infant were up at the podium. The prisoner smiled at her, and started to rustle in his chains as he moved toward her before the guards instantly came over to stop him. She blew him a kiss, and her toddler mumbled "Da da."

That's when my eyes made out the tattoo on the back of his neck. It was a dragon—identical to hers. I heard a racing heartbeat and a quickening pulse. It wasn't my client's—it was mine. The sound grew louder—a page out of Edgar Allen Poe's telltale heart—as the probation officer listed the young man's lifetime of crimes. He'd been on juvenile probation in New Mexico. He then committed adult crimes in another state. His juvenile probation violation of "failing to report" was the least of his worries in light of the adult crimes of armed robbery, attempted murder and aggravated mayhem, whatever that was. Unfortunately, his juvenile warrant had never been addressed until now.

Somewhere in the "in and out" of the prisoner's criminal history, I realized that the young man had probably been right here in town the night that Christina had come back to my place. He was probably the "someone" she had left me to see. I thought of a half-a-dozen horror movies of my own. Had his demons passed through to her and then onto my lap?

I looked around at the tough crowd around me—the boys in undershirts, their mothers in halter tops. I couldn't feel superior to them anymore. Did I really think that I could enter the dark places of the Earth and still emerge as white as my client's polo shirt?

Up in front of the judge, Christina grew bored after the recounting of the disposition of the second aggravation in Amarillo. She scanned the courtroom and our eyes met for a brief moment with a glimmer of recognition, before she turned away.

Had she mentioned me to him? Did she have even the slightest idea who I was? Or was I just another potential one night stand? As she turned her rapt attention back at him, there was no question.

I felt a nudge, which drew me back into the courtroom. My client's mother looked at me with a disappointed look—

she expected me to say something to her boy, his expression seemed all wrong. He didn't look at the prisoner at all; his eyes were locked on Christina. He wasn't scared straight, he was being turned on.

"Just imagine that guy as your cellmate," I started awkwardly, whispering into his ear. "If you screw up again, you could be sharing a cell with him!"

My client nodded vaguely as the image formed in his mind. "If you said the wrong thing. Let's say you made a joke about his pretty little girlfriend there, he would tear you apart. I don't have to tell you what else he would do to you."

I didn't have to spell it out. My client squirmed under the weight of my sudden intensity. "Take a good look at them. You don't want to live in their world! You might think you're being cool, hanging out with people like that, but it is not a place that you can handle!"

I took another breath, I then nearly spit in his face like a drill sergeant. "Trust me on this!"

My client cringed. Sweat stained his forehead. He closed his eyes. He was making a choice, or perhaps saying a prayer. His mother smiled at me, her eyes then turned heavenward with thanks. This is exactly what she wanted. He whispered something in her ear, and she looked over at me. It was time to go, the message had been sent.

Christina was about to speak on the prisoner's behalf as we shuffled out of the courtroom. We shut the door behind us, very, very quietly so as not to disturb her, or him.

"We certainly got our money's worth," the mother said. "Thank you and thank God!"

Her son was still shaking. "I don't think I want to come back here. Ever!"

"You know what," I said, forcing a lame smile. "Neither

do I!"

They laughed as they walked past the metal detectors out into the daylight. I waited around for a few minutes until court recessed. Christina walked past me, the infant amazingly quiet. I gathered that this sentencing went as well as could be expected. She still had his "adult" sentencing downtown tomorrow, and I guess the one in Texas a couple of weeks after that.

"Good luck" was all that I could think of to say. She looked much younger now that tears streaked her make-up. She was just a young woman stuck in a bad relationship for the next ten years, five with good time.

"Thank you," she softly said and left. I knew I would never see her again.

Much like Malcolm McDowell at the end of *Clockwork Orange*, I was cured.

For now ...

(AFI Networks Newsletter)

THE NEUTRON STORY ON THE FIRST DATE

"Don't tell the neutron story," I said to myself for the hundredth time as I delved into my Cajun shrimp pasta. I stared at my date as we had dinner in at the "Ragin' Shrimp" restaurant— my standard $12.95 a plate first date joint with its black and white pictures of New Orleans on the white walls. Other than the phone call, I'd known her for all of five minutes. She was an English teacher from my home town of Albuquerque, with the exotic name of Jasmine. My father knew her from a mutual friend and had described her as a "keeper." Now this "keeper" ate crawfish on white rice as I asked her about the "rewards of teaching at a private as opposed to a public school."

She mumbled something about "small class size."

I bit my tongue. "Don't tell her the neutron story!" I thought for the hundred and first time. "It's too risky!"

Every writer has a "neutron story" in his arsenal. Like the ultra-classified neutron bomb, it's potent yet unstable combination of humor, pathos and a dash of sex, designed to totally penetrate the defenses of the listener. The desired target objective was either a movie deal or romance. Sometimes both.

My neutron story has never been written down, much less published, to prevent it from falling into enemy hands. In Hollywood meetings, the neutron story had helped my novel get published, and then get it optioned by a production company. In e-mail, the neutron story had even inspired a beautiful model to drive across the desert, up the two hundred mile route the Spanish had named *Jornada del Muerto*, just to have lunch with me.

In its pure form, the story involves ten years, four women, (but only two sex scenes), and three carefully placed jokes at the end of each act. There's the R-rated version and the G-rated version, a male version and a female version, and the "cocktail party prototype." It can take thirty seconds in the telling, or if I don't watch out, it can take over an hour.

For every success, there had been the misfires — the second joke can be risky in mixed company. Like the B-52 loaded with nukes in *Dr. Strangelove,* once I begin, I pretty much lose all communication links. I cannot be recalled. There had been collateral damage in earlier versions.

I took my tenth sip of iced tea and now had more brown tea in my blood stream than red blood cells. She drank merlot; her lips grew red and moist as we talked. We had gone to neighboring high schools, and she even mentioned hanging out with an old girlfriend of mine back when they were on the Eldorado High School swim team. I wisely avoided any follow-up about the old girlfriend.

"Don't talk about old relationships," I thought. "Women hate that."

She now coached Girls' Swimming at the private school, and I couldn't help but ask her "What's your favorite stroke?"

She grimaced. Bad move on my part. So tacky.

She was attractive enough, intelligent enough. She brushed my hand when I dropped my fork on the ground and picked it up, and then smiled.

She mentioned something about admiring great writers because of their "dedication to their art. She was an English teacher and all that. Perhaps she was a keeper, yet we seemed to be at an impasse. It could go either way.

Then she threw me the opening. "So tell me how you wrote your book?" She said, tilting her head forward. "I bet that's a story in itself."

I couldn't help myself. We had pretty much exhausted Girl's Swimming, and mutual friends. I didn't want to drop any more silverware. I had no more alternatives—I felt the neutron story rise out of my gut like the monster in *Alien*.

I tried to stop the launch. "It's a long story, a really long story."

"I'd really love to hear it," She took another sip of merlot, as if opening a door, or was it a trapdoor? "Maybe you could lecture to my class sometime."

She had me at the word "really." I was soon in the midst of the full-bore, R-rated, neutron story. After the line "She's fictional, I'm Jewish. Just think what the kids would be," it was too late. Once I got to Act III and "What's that red beating thing in the trash, oh I'm sorry, it's my heart" and "I don't know whether I said that line to her or wrote it in the book," it was all over.

I finished, an hour might have passed for all I knew. She might have gone to the bathroom in the middle of the story, but I hadn't even noticed.

She stared at me for a second, as if assessing the damage. She was still standing. But what was going on inside?

She took another deep breath, and then looked at the waiter. She chugged the last of the merlot and wiped her face. "We'll take separate checks."

She handed a credit card, and looked at me accusingly until I forked over some cash, kept looking until I added an extra five bucks for the tip. She mumbled something about "an early class tomorrow," and within instants, she was out the door, vaporized. I stared at the empty seat in front of me and swore softly to myself. How many times did I have to tell myself—don't tell the neutron story on a first date?

SUNSET BLUES

The first time it happened, I was on the real Sunset Boulevard in Los Angeles, sitting in a house that some golden-age actress could have died in. I talked with my wildly successful cousin at his home, rambling on about my first victorious jury trial. The fact that he was working as a television agent was certainly at the back of my mind.

I pitched the story about a teenager accused of trying to blow up his high school. I won the case with a great sound bite – *"Where there's smoke, there's reasonable doubt."* According to the expert witnesses, the chemicals in question were not harmful, and I sold that point to the jury.

"Couldn't you just picture that 'where's the smoke' line, in one of your prime time legal dramas?" I asked him eagerly.

He nodded, took another call and nodded to someone on the phone.

The conversation switched to some other topics when the phone rang again. Surprisingly enough it was for me.

It was an old friend of mine who got the number from my office. "Your client, the arson one," she said. "He was mixing chemicals and things went wrong. He's dead."

I do not know if it was the same chemicals, whether it was suicide or an accident. I didn't want to know. As the sun set into the overbearing smog, I wanted to quit law, quit writing about law. Suddenly, where there was smoke, there was a dead seventeen year old boy.

I'd been a public defender at the time of the meeting.

155

When I returned home to my office, I talked with my supervisor, who told me "Welcome to the club." He had a client who had hung himself, the day before an appeals court had granted a new trial. We both went out that night to a blues club, commiserated. We then both went back to work the next day. My new client was a battered woman accused of perjury, with eighteen months on the line.

A few years later, when I was on my own, I was appointed as a guardian ad litem for two young children who were being taken away from their mother for abuse and neglect. The young children were adorable and very smart for their ages. They lived in a rural county near the big city, the kind of place where the Unabomber would live if he only wanted to be an hour away from a Walmart.

The mother was represented by a passionate new lawyer. Over the course of the year of the case, he fought hard for his client, truly believed in her. I didn't like him much at the time because he was so zealous and battled on even the smallest of points.

Over the course of the year, the woman made real changes in her life. She kicked drugs, got a job, and got away from bad relationships. According to the social worker, a tough judge of character from dealing with all the kids of the area; the woman had successfully completed treatment and was now capable of caring for the children. Her lawyer presented letters from employers and therapists attesting to her breakthrough.

I talked with my clients and their foster mother. All agreed that it was in the children's best interests to return to their mother. So on a sunny day, filled with hugs on all sides, the mother regained custody.

In the months that followed both the children and their

mother made excellent progress—the social worker said they were happy, and they were doing well in school. Placement stayed with the mother. The mother's lawyer was justifiably proud of his efforts; I congratulated him and told him he'd done a great job. We had a happy ending for a change.

I spoke too soon of course.

While speeding to take the children to counseling, there was an accident. They all died. I don't know the details.

I ran into the young lawyer a few days after the accident. He was still in tears. He blamed himself, because he had once seen the woman drive quickly, passing him on the way back from Court.

I told him that I drove quickly; I passed him coming back from court as well, because he drove forty miles an hour. Speed wasn't the issue. He had done his job, we all had. There was no way we could ever know exactly what happened in the accident, and whose fault it was. But based on the available information at the hearing, months earlier, we had both done what justice had required.

And for about six months, we had been correct.

He still couldn't stop wiping his eyes. He told me that he still would have argued for the woman, that he still believed her. She hadn't failed. He had.

I put my hand on his shoulder. Before he could go back to the speeding, I looked him in the eye.

"Being a good lawyer is like being a blues guitarist," I said, remembering my talk with my own supervisor. "You have to have feeling and sensitivity in your fingers and your heart. In order to feel the passion and play hard, but you have to develop calluses too or you will bleed all the time and you won't be able to play anymore."

I still feel for my clients, I will always fight for them, but when they go down, I don't go down with them. I have to be there for the next one after all.

After every sunset, there's a sunrise.

(East Mountain Independent)

DEATH OF A YOUNG LAWYER

According to the official rules of the American Bar Association, you officially stop being a "young lawyer" on your 36th birthday. In my early thirties, I had already noticed more and more hairs were left in the drain after every shower, but I was still thirty-five when I stopped being young, stopped being a lawyer, and nearly stopped being alive.

"The presumption of innocence is green" is an old criminal lawyer's adage. Fade in to my sparse basement office, talking to a young man facing hard time for a crime, a serious case coupled with his serious lack of presumption.

I visibly hesitated when he mentioned that he didn't have any money whatsoever for a retainer. There was a reason that my office looked like a dorm room, and that reason was green.

Before I could decline the case, he told me he'd heard great things about me. I had a great reputation as a "lawyer who really cared." I smiled, but flattery wasn't enough to get me out of the dorm.

He then promised me I'd get his bond, worth several thousand dollars once the case was concluded. "Several" and "thousand" were two words I did like. I saw the gentleman standing right there in front of me, I made the presumption that he did indeed have a bond and that several thousand dollars would soon be mine after only a few weeks of work.

The man stared at me. "This is the type of case that could make you *the man*."

Being "the man" sure sounded good at the time. We shook hands on it, but didn't put anything down in writing. I was going to be the dashing Mathew McConnaghey in the adaptation of John Grisham's *A Time to Kill,* though technically this story would be: *A Time to Aggravated Batter With a Deadly Weapon (Firearm Enhancement).*

Dissolve to series of scenes—a few weeks of preparation, then another week of hard-fought jury trial. The twelve angry men and women came back happy when it was over. With the help of able co-counsel we had triumphed and my client was acquitted of almost everything except a relatively minor probation violation. My cross-examination of the cop was readily becoming the stuff of legends.

I had made another presumption before the court that day—victory. I had already drafted the "Order to Release Bond" for the judge to sign. Right as the judge was about to call it a wrap, I handed it to him. He smiled at me, signed the order immediately, right up there on the bench. I assumed that I would wake up the next morning a wealthy man. End of Act I.

Fade into the next morning and the ACT II inciting incident. When I got to work at dawn the next morning, a voice on my answering machine that sounded vaguely like Clint Eastwood in one of his Dirty Harry roles, said that I was dead, although not in those exact words.

The voice continued. I found out that my client had not been the one who had posted the bond. It was his brother, the possessor of the angry Clint voice, and Clint had expected that his money was damn sure going to be returned to its rightful owner.

By the way, did I mention that a quick computer check revealed that Clint had indeed gone to prison for turning a former living person into a dead person?

In utter panic, I went to the District Attorney's Office and they recorded the call. I think I actually said "Are you getting this?" to the investigators in the middle of the call. Clint was no dummy, so he managed to avoid direct threats while we were on the phone. He vaguely mentioned reporting the whole thing to the disciplinary board.

Close in shot on the ADA. He frowned. There hadn't been anything concrete on the recording, and if I had indeed failed due diligence, I was on my own. Just like Gary Cooper as the hero of *High Noon*, without the being heroic part.

Smash-cut to me walking out into a windy parking lot, shivering, cursing. I didn't have a posse to back me up. I certainly couldn't ask my dad for help on this one. I thought back to the phone call he'd made to a teacher when the cool kids in ninth grade had thrown my lock in the urinal. My father's phone call certainly wouldn't dissuade a man like Clint.

When I got back to my office, there was yet another message on my machine. Clint needed the money by the end of the week. He was marginally nicer because he realized that he needed me alive … for the moment. He realized that the check may have been made out to him, but the court could only release the check to me. We made some hurried negotiations, he in that deep biblical baritone. In my mumbling I hoped I sounded like Marlin Brando in *The Godfather*. I mumbled a starting offer, and then quickly caved in to his offer—I would get to keep a third of the money if I could get it to him soon. I guess my negotiating skills would qualify me as a loser in professional circles. Still, even though I would still end up losing on the deal, I would be a live loser as opposed to a dead one.

Or so I hoped. I had his word on it that he'd let me live. Just like I had his friend's word that I'd get paid. Great! I closed my eyes. A million bloodbaths from a million movies flashed through my head. Sirens flashed.

I opened my eyes, the message light on my phone was still flashing. I pressed play. My client's probation officer needed to see me about a pre-sentence report on the misdemeanors.

As I called the probation officer back, a vague plan came into my head. I asked him if he'd do a little favor for me. By the way, did I mention that this officer had played semi-professional football and was permitted to carry a loaded firearm? Firearm enhancements work both ways.

The next day, the probation officer reluctantly drove me to the courthouse in a state car. When I went to the bonding office on the fourth floor, the harried clerk was extremely suspicious when I said my name.

"We've had two people claiming to be Jonathan Miller already this morning," she said. "Three yesterday. You should see the woman claiming to be your wife."

I had to show two forms of ID and my bar card before he handed me the check. I noticed a large gentleman in an Oakland Raiders shirt speak into a cell phone as I walked out the door.

I sprinted out to the waiting car. Safe … for the moment.

We then drove to Clint's place of business. The probation officer made his fantasy football picks over his intercom. He didn't mention to his dispatcher where he was going.

I was too scared to reply when he asked whether he should use Baltimore's kicker or Buffalo's.

The Final Conflict of Act III. Extreme Close-up on Clint's hard face, impatiently waiting in the parking lot. The probation officer dropped me off and waited in the parking lot, he kept the motor running.

"Don't be a wimp," I mumbled to myself. I shook like a leaf as Clint came toward me. I showed him the wilted check in my sweaty hand. He didn't look armed, but then again he didn't open his Oakland Raiders jacket.

He glanced at the state car, said nothing, and then motioned to the bank across the street. Under the watchful eye of the probation officer, we crossed over and headed inside the bank.

Inside, the line was long, real long. How many films had there been about botched bank robberies?

An old lady complained to the teller. Clint grew agitated, as did I. He swore under his breath, something about death yet again. Finally, a teller motioned him over. I handed him the check and he gave it to the cashier. After a few slow-motion moments, she handed him the money, then he gave me my share in crisp hundred bills. The bank guard looked at us both suspiciously, but we were already out the door.

I hurried to the probation officer's car, told him to get driving. He was still talking to his dispatcher.

"Go with the guy from Buffalo," I said. "Let's get the hell out of here."

Clint was still inside as we turned off onto San Mateo Boulevard in Albuquerque. He might have stayed behind to rob the place for all I knew, or cared.

When I arrived at home, I took a deep breath then showered until I had washed every ounce of sweat out of my body. When I turned off the shower, I noticed even more hairs then usual clogging the drain ...

After I turned thirty-six, I moved out to Los Angeles to get a Master's in Fine Arts in Screenwriting at the American

Film Institute. Some of my Los Angeles adventures can be found in the *Amarillo in August* collection. Right before I turned thirty-eight, on the day I graduated from AFI, my first novel, *Rattlesnake Lawyer* was published by Cool Titles, a small independent press based in Beverly Hills.

I thought my life would finally settle down when my novel was finally published. I was wrong … .

To be continued …

ABOUT JONATHAN MILLER

 Jonathan Miller has practiced criminal defense law all over New Mexico. He currently practices in Albuquerque where he writes and stays active in legal services that help the poor. Jon is a graduate of Albuquerque Academy, Cornell University, the University of Colorado School of Law, and the American Film Institute. He also wrote for the syndicated TV show *Arrest and Trial* and hopes to use his writing royalties to pay off his student loans before he dies.

Jon's books, Crater County and Amarillo in August both made the Tucson public library's master list of Southwestern books of the year, Volcano Verdict was a finalist for New Mexico mystery of the year, and his book *LaBajada Lawyer* is a finalist in the 2010 ForeWord book awards for Multi-Cultural Fiction.

RECENT CASA DE SNAPDRAGON RELEASES

One Calamitous Spring
Edward F. Mendez
Paperback ISBN: 9781937240356
eBook ISBN: 9781937240363

Theodora Mercedes has deep Santa Fe roots but her focus is on the present and tomorrow, and not on where she looks, but in what she sees. Making a better world, creating a stronger family, and paying attention to the universe that gives her life are where she puts her energies.

My Magic Cowboy
Katy Lente
Paperback ISBN: 9781937240264
eBook ISBN: 9781937240332

As budding anthropologist, Carly Brumley, enters her junior year in high school, she continues the slow process of healing from the loss of her beloved little brother, Cord. She employs a big gray Quarter Horse, raised and broken by her uncle, to help her regain her passion for riding. Carly's artistic boyfriend, Danny O'Hara, carefully pushes his way, along with his secret, into the center of Carly's world.

Serenity and Beauty
Rita Mosiman
Hardcover ISBN: 9781937240196

As an avid hiker feeling a strong connection to the land and nature's artistry, I decided to create an art book, which will hopefully assuage the gloomy clouds of recent global economic woes. Nature is inspiring, soothing, exciting, and powerful. It helps us to remember that true beauty in life exists in the simplest of things, which reach every soul open to them if only we look, sense, and feel.

Over Exposed
Terri Muuss
Paperback ISBN: 9781937240233
eBook ISBN: 9781937240240

In the pages that follow, Muuss brings us close to what we might describe as the secret war, the intimate war, which resides in closed rooms, in seemingly ordinary homes. Yet these poems are written, reader, with such delicacy, such concern for image, for pause, and purpose-for, in fact, beauty.

Made in the USA
San Bernardino, CA
01 April 2014